AF482132

A COLONIAL ADVOCATE

*The Launching of his Newspaper
and the Queenston Career of
William Lyon Mackenzie*

PUBLISHER
Curiosity House
190 Mill Street, Box 308,
Creemore, Ontario, Canada L0M 1G0
in association with
Mackenzie Heritage Printery Museum
Box 1824, Queenston, Ontario L0S 1L0
and
Clan MacKenzie Society of Canada
580 Rebecca Street
Oakville, Ontario L6K 3N9

Printed in Canada by Premier Impressions, Inc.

A portion of this book originally appeared in slightly different form in
The Beaver magazine April–May, 1999.

CANADIAN CATALOGING IN PUBLICATION DATA
Raible, Chris, 1933–
    A colonial advocate: the launching of his newspaper and the
Queenston career of William Lyon Mackenzie

Includes bibliographical references
ISBN 0-9696418-1-8

    1. Mackenzie, William Lyon, 1795-1861. 2. Colonial Advocate Press.
3. Ontario – History – 1791-1841. 4. Canadian newspapers – History –
19th century. I. Mackenzie Heritage Printery Museum.
II. Clan MacKenzie Society of Canada. II. Title.

FC451.M33R35 1999   971.03'6   C99-900456-5
F1032.R24 199

A COLONIAL ADVOCATE

*The Launching of his Newspaper
and the Queenston Career
of William Lyon Mackenzie*

by Chris Raible

CURIOSITY HOUSE — CREEMORE, ONTARIO
*for The Mackenzie Heritage Printery Museum
and The Clan MacKenzie Society of Canada*

Acknowledgements

The Mackenzie Heritage Printery Committee and the Clan MacKenzie Society would like to thank the following individuals and companies for their contributions in producing *A Colonial Advocate: The Launching of his Newspaper and the Queenston Career of William Lyon Mackenzie*:

- Chris Raible for his generous donation of the manuscript contained herein.
- Canadian Paper Trade Association for their gift of the paper used in the production of the book.
- Premier Impressions Inc. of Grimsby, Ontario for the filmwork and printing of the book.
- And, last but not least, Van Huizen Bookbinding and Finishing of St. Catharines, Ontario for binding and finishing what the reader now holds.

A Few Words from the
Mackenzie Heritage Printery Committee

THE MACKENZIE HERITAGE PRINTERY MUSEUM, located in Queenston, Ontario, in the restored home of firebrand editor William Lyon Mackenzie, is Canada's only working printing museum. It is a joint venture between the Niagara Parks Commission and the Mackenzie Printery Committee, a not-for profit group concerned with preserving vintage printing equipment and raising public awareness of the contributions of printing to Canada's economic, social and cultural development.

On May 18, 1824 William Lyon Mackenzie published the first issue of the *Colonial Advocate* in Queenston, and with it began a career of public activism towards the reformation of the government of Upper Canada.

By the mid-1930s, the only remnants of the home's former glory were skeletal remains of the walls and a single small stone marker, erected by the Niagara Historical Society, which proclaimed "Home of William Lyon Mackenzie. The birthplace of responsible government, 1823-24."

In 1936 the Niagara Parks Commission undertook the restoration of the Mackenzie House and the rebuilt home was officially opened on June 18, 1938 by Prime Minister William Lyon Mackenzie King.

The original plan for the restored home was to house a printing museum:

> The Queenston printing plant in which William Lyon Mackenzie published the preliminary blasts in his campaign for responsible government in Canada is to 'live' again…. Presses of the type employed by the old Niagara area 'rebel' will be obtained for the reconstructed building, giving tourists a definite picture of the historic shop.
>
> ST. CATHARINES STANDARD, 1936

Unfortunately these plans were put off, and such heritage preservation and perpetuation did not take place until 1991. Discussions began between the Mackenzie Heritage Printery Committee and the Niagara Parks Commission. The Printery Committee assembled a collection of working heritage presses and an interpretive display on the history of printing, and the museum opened for its inaugural season. Leadership and initial funding was provided by Henry Burgoyne and Al Teather of the Burgoyne Newspaper Group based in St. Catharines.

From these plans, formulated almost ten years ago, the volunteer Printery Committee and the Niagara Parks Commission continue a successful operating partnership. The Commission owns and operates the museum, while the Volunteer Committee oversees and maintains the museum collection and secures necessary funding.

The collection has grown to include eight working presses, hot type technology, including an operating Linotype and Ludlow type casters, and a lithography workshop. Demonstrations of the operating equipment encourage hands-on experience for the visitor.

The gem of the museum's collection is an English common press, known as the Louis Roy, that is believed to be the oldest press in Canada. Built in England in the 1760s, it was acquired by Lieutenant-Governor John Graves Simcoe to print Upper Canada's first newspaper, *The Upper Canada Gazette and American Oracle*, in Newark (Niagara-on-the-Lake), April 17, 1793.

Each year the Mackenzie Printery mounts an informative and educational exhibit that helps to illustrate the variety of ways that printing touches our lives. As the Mackenzie Heritage Printery Museum enters its ninth season of operation, we are returning to explore and celebrate our roots with the 1999 exhibit, "William Lyon Mackenzie Rebel Editor: the 175th Anniversary of the Colonial Advocate."

A Few Words from the
Clan MacKenzie Society

THE CLAN MACKENZIE SOCIETY IN THE AMERICAS, Canadian Chapter is a registered Canadian charity which has as one of its objectives: "to encourage, educate and foster an interest in the history and cultural heritage of the MacKenzie Clan; the Highland Clans in general and their relationships with the history of Scotland, Canada and the rest of the world." We were, therefore, very pleased to have an opportunity to become involved with the publication of Chris Raible's book on William Lyon Mackenzie in conjunction with our good friends at the Mackenzie Heritage Printery Museum.

William Lyon Mackenzie is one of those giants of Canadian history for whom we have a sneaking admiration. He attacked the corruption which had become endemic in the society of Upper Canada in the early 19th century. As a consequence he earned the displeasure of high-ranking people in high places and in those days that was either a brave or a foolhardy thing to do. Leading the Rebellion of 1837 led to a price on his head of £1,000. But one is always attracted to the little guy who stands up to the powerful bully, the David to the Goliath, or the honest man to the crook. The "Little Rebel" was such a man.

The MacKenzies come from the vast county of Ross & Cromarty in the Highlands of Scotland. They seem to have been big supporters of the House of Stewart and many supported Bonnie Prince Charlie in his ill-fated effort at Culloden in 1746 to seize back the crown for his father, the erstwhile King James III & VIII. But it failed and many Mackenzies who supported the Stewarts were transported. William Lyon Mackenzie claimed that both his grandfathers were at Culloden, which may well have been the case.

The Clan MacKenzie Society in Canada has around 1,000 members. The Canadian telephone directories list over 14,000 with that name. Membership is open to all and costs a modest $15 a year. Enquiries for membership can be made to Clan MacKenzie Society, c/o Alan McKenzie, FSAScot, 580 Rebecca Street, Oakville, Ontario L6K 3N9, or e-mail: alanmck@cgocable.net

Table of Topic Headings

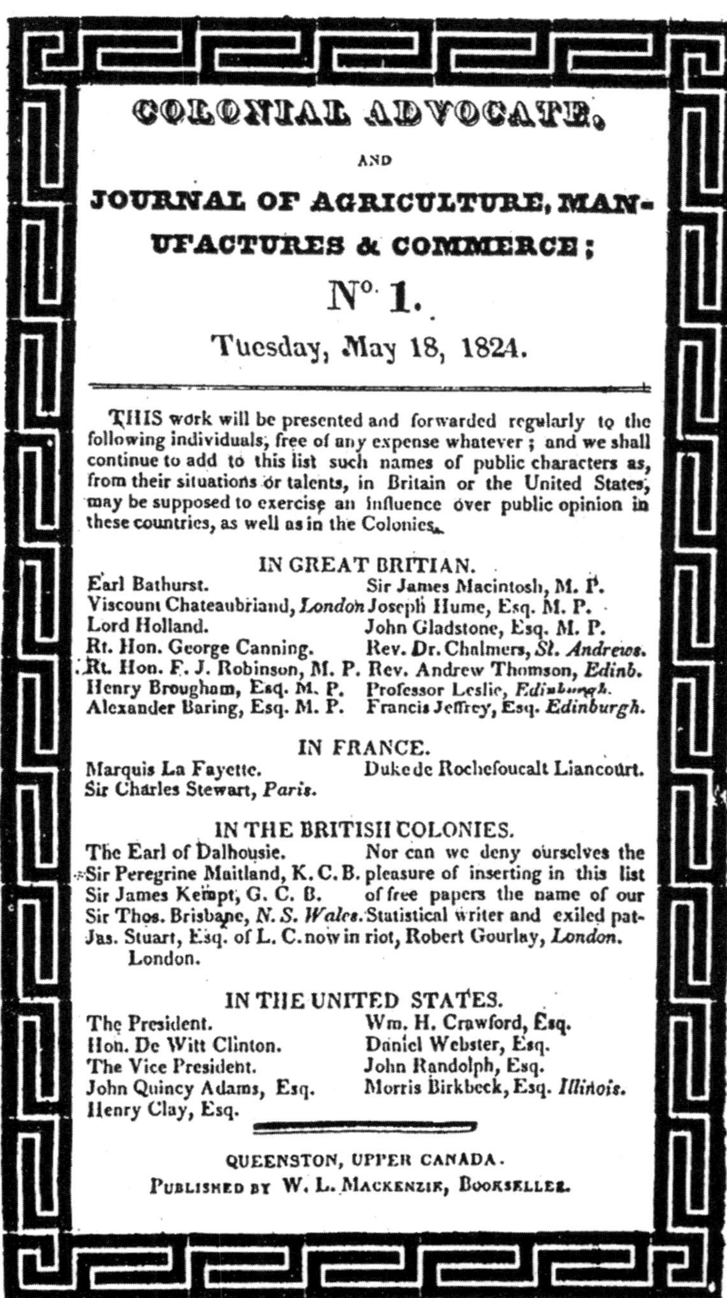

The front page of the first issue of the Colonial Advocate.

Mackenzie's Early Life

Launching the 'Advocate'

N MAY 18, 1824 WILLIAM LYON MACKENZIE produced the first issue of a new publication, the *Colonial Advocate*. His purpose was nothing less than the political reformation of Upper Canada.

A total political unknown, the new editor rashly affirmed his intention "to discuss the merits of public men and public measures, with a freedom and plainness rather unusual in the greater part of our colonial publications."[1]

In that first issue, he boldly declared:

❧ Money is in the hands of a few of the persons in the government employ, and in the hands of nobody else.

❧ We [will] investigate the cause of [Lieutenant-Governor] Sir Peregrine Maitland's inactivity.…We will carefully go over the principal matters connected with his administration…for the present we cannot remember anything he has done of a public nature worth recording.

❧ We want churchmen who would come up to, or nearly to the picture of a gospel minister…lovers more of the flock, than of the fleece.

❧ Far be it from us to desire to bring into disrepute the government of this country; yet we will not fail to point out their errors. Ridicule shall not be spared: it may effect our purpose when grave argument would fail.

❧ We would fain hope that…some of the cursed restrictions which short-sighted stupid party minded legislatures, have enacted to fetter, to choke, to destroy the trade, and cramp the exertions of the country may be put down and set at naught.

❧ It is the system we condemn…the system of cross-purposes that the colonies are governed by"

As his biographer would write nearly forty years later, "Something new under the sun had appeared in the newspaper world of Upper Canada."[2] The *Colonial Advocate* may not have been the first independent newspaper in Upper Canada, nor was it the first to attack the government; but it was the first such paper to do so effectively and survive – eventually to succeed both as a political venture and as a commercial enterprise.

Producing the first *Advocate* issues and dealing with the early public response became, in a sense, a prologue to the drama of the rest of Mackenzie's life. In Queenston he produced some twenty issues of his newspaper before, in the fall of 1824, he moved his publishing enterprise to the provincial capital, York (later Toronto), and to the colourful career which earned him his place in Canadian history.

The first issue of the *Advocate* began with lines from the Scottish editor's favourite poet, Robert Burns:

> O Scotia! my dear, my native soil!
> For whom my warmest wish to heaven is sent!
> Long may thy hardy sons of rustic toil,
> Be blest with health and peace and sweet content!
>
> And O! may heav'n their simple lives prevent
> From luxury's contagion, weak and vile!
> Then, howe'er Crowns and Coronets be rent,
> A virtuous Populace may rise the while,
> And stand a wall of fire around their much lov'd isle.
>   *"Cotter's Saturday Night"*

By quoting these lines, Mackenzie revealed himself to be more of a democrat than he may have realized. Democracy was a dirty word in Upper Canada. It was synonymous with Yankee republicanism. Anyone with democratic sympathies, even if clothed in Scottish dress, was bound to be dismissed as being too American. The editor tried to head off such an attack by dissociating himself from any suggestion that he wished to remake Upper Canada in the image of the United States:

> We would never wish to see British America an appendage of the
> American Presidency; yet would we wish to see British America thrive
> and prosper full well as does that Presidency.... We like American liberty
> well, but greatly prefer British liberty. British subjects, born in Britain, we
> have sworn allegiance to a constitutional monarchy, and we will die
> before we will violate that oath.

(Ironically, Mackenzie later did violate that oath. In 1837, following the failure of the Rebellion, he escaped to the United States. A few years later, in exile and with little hope of ever again living in Canada, he became an American citizen, forswearing all foreign allegiances.[3] In 1850 the rebel returned with his family to Canada — thanks to the amnesty proclaimed a year earlier — and reassumed his former status as a British subject.)

Mackenzie's Life Before the 'Colonial Advocate'

Launching the *Colonial Advocate* was an audacious act. The editor had been in Canada less than four years. There is nothing in his personal history prior that time to suggest that he was destined for a career as a crusading journalist or as a reform politician, much less as a radical revolutionary.

In his native Scotland, Mackenzie had been a shopkeeper. Born in 1795 in Dundee, he was moderately well educated and was apprenticed for a commercial career as an accountant and an apothecary.[4] At the age of eighteen, with his mother's support and assistance, he opened a general store in Alyth, a village a few miles from Dundee. Had that Alyth business enterprise not gone bankrupt in 1816 in the severe economic depression which followed the Napoleonic wars,[5] Mackenzie might never have left Scotland.

After a subsequent similar shop failure back in Dundee, Mackenzie went south, obtaining work in England. The exact nature of his employment is not known, save that bookkeeping and mathematical skills were required and that some of his time was spent working for companies constructing canals. In 1820, like many from his homeland seeking a fresh start, he emigrated to Canada.

In Canada, after a brief initial period working on the Lachine canal, Mackenzie resumed his entrepreneurial pursuits. For the first time in his life, he began to make money. In partnership with his Dundee friend John Lesslie (whose father's capital initially funded the enterprise), Mackenzie operated highly successful general stores, first in York and then in Dundas. The two advertised themselves as "Mackenzie and Lesslie Druggists, and Dealers in Hardware, Cutlery, Jewelry, Toys, Carpenter's Tools, Nails, Groceries, Confections, Dye Stuffs, Paints, &., at the Circulating Library, Dundas."[6] Sometime in 1822, Mackenzie and Lesslie had a falling out. The exact reasons are unclear, but they may have had something to do with Mackenzie's dropping an interest in Lesslie's sister.[7] When the partnership dissolved, Mackenzie purchased the assets for the considerable sum of £686.19s. 3 ½p.[8]

That same year Mackenzie's mother, Elizabeth, along with the woman she had selected to be his wife, Isabel Baxter, arrived in Canada from Scotland. With them was Mackenzie's eight-year-old natural son, James, whom Elizabeth had reared from infancy.[9] Mackenzie met them all in Montreal in June, 1822 – three weeks later the couple were married.

Mackenzie brought his new family to Dundas where he continued to keep shop. Something more than a year later, they moved to Queenston where he opened a new store, advertising himself as "Grocer, Druggist and Haberdasher."[10] He also sold books on a wide range of subjects (in the first issue of the *Colonial Advocate*, he identified himself as "W. L. Mackenzie, Bookseller")

In the spring of 1824, while much occupied with launching his newspaper, Mackenzie still continued his other business enterprises. Along with his Queenston store he busily supplied goods to his old friend Thomas Fyfe who had opened a general store in Esquesing.[11] In Canada, in contrast to Scotland, Mackenzie was clearly making a reasonably good living. He could accurately confess: "We are not in want, neither are we rich."

(In keeping with his Scottish heritage, throughout his life money was always important to him. Much of his Dundee apprenticeship involved accounting. During his later Canadian political career, he often challenged the government over its waste of money, backing his arguments with detailed accounting figures.[12] Through all his endeavours, he kept careful track of money – the amounts owed to him and the amounts of his own indebtedness – even during his all-too-frequent periods of financial difficulty.)[13]

Neither Mackenzie's Scottish years nor his first years in Canada offer hints of any revolutionary spirit. His native Dundee may have had a reputation as a "radical toun," as a centre of sympathy for the French Revolution, and as a place of popular demonstrations of dissatisfaction with the government,[14] but Mackenzie was not personally involved.[15] Later in his life, while revisiting his birthplace in 1833, he would recall that "from my boyhood upwards I was fond of politics,"[16] but there was no public evidence of that interest. If in Dundee, as near the end of his life he asserted, he first "imbibed…ideas of freedom, justice and progress,"[17] prior to 1824 that ingestion found no public expression.

To the contrary, in his first *Advocate* editorial he reassured his readers that "we have never been disloyal subjects nor radical reformers; we have neither joined Spa-fields mobs [protest demonstrations in London in 1816], nor benefited by the harangues of [radical journalists] Hunt, Cobbett and Watson."[18]

After his arrival in Canada Mackenzie showed some political curiosity, but not very much. In 1821 (he had been in York five months) he watched from the gallery as the Upper Canada Assembly elected its Speaker.[19] Shortly after his move to Dundas he acted as secretary at a public meeting at which "resolutions were adopted favorable to Canadian Manufactures."[20] What effect the resolutions had, if any, is not recorded. Not until he moved to Queenston did he hold public office – shortly after the launching of the *Advocate* he was elected a trustee of the village school.[21]

Nor were there many hints that he would one day embark on an editorial enterprise. It is clear, even from his earliest years in school, that he devoured the written word. He was an avid reader of *The Dundee, Perth, and Cupar Advertiser* – he once boasted that he had been the youngest member of that newspaper's reading room.[22] He loved books. From age eleven to age twenty-three, he kept track of all the books he read – some 956 titles in religion, history, geography, science, literature.[23] As a teenager in Dundee, he helped found a "rational society" for the encouragement of scientific study and debate.[24]

One biography claims that, before coming to Canada, Mackenzie wrote for a London newspaper[25] – if so, it is strange that Mackenzie himself made no mention of it. His only known published piece in England was strictly non-political: a sketch of a disabled mechanical genius Mackenzie had known in Alyth.[26] The same biography asserts that soon after coming to Canada Mackenzie contributed to the York newspaper, the *Observer*, under the pseudonym "Mercator" – if so, no copy is extant.[27]

Thus, prior to putting out the *Colonial Advocate*, Mackenzie had published virtually nothing.[28] As he acknowledged in that first issue, he had "not written for the press before" and his "character and talents as a writer are but little known." Apart from his extensive reading, he knew little about editing, less about publishing and nothing whatever about printing. Nonetheless, he announced his intention to "come forward to controvert received opinions, and to offer views which have previously passed unnoticed."

Marketing the 'Advocate'

By his selecting the name "Colonial Advocate," Mackenzie assumed the role of advocate, of spokesman, for the British colonist – for the people, not for the Government:

> We conceive ourselves as independent as editors well can be….We have never been disloyal subjects nor radical reformers. But we have made our election: it is to have only one patron, and that patron is the People: – the people of the British Colonies.

Launching the *Advocate* demonstrated that Mackenzie was nothing if not sure of himself. He fully expected his paper to be read by men in prominent political positions, "public characters as, from their situations or talents…may be supposed to exercise an influence over public opinion in [their] countries, as well as in the Colonies."

To indicate how serious were his political intentions (and revealing how large was his sense of self-importance), he listed, on the front cover of the first issue of the *Advocate*, the men to whom his paper would "be presented and forwarded regularly…free of any expense whatever." It was quite a list:

IN GREAT BRITAIN

Earl Bathurst.[29]	Sir James Macintosh, M.P.[30]
Viscount Chateaubriand London.[31]	Joseph Hume, Esq. M.P.[32]
Lord Holland.[33]	John Gladstone, Esq. M.P.[34]
Rt. Hon. George Canning.[35]	Rev. Dr. Chalmers, St. Andrews.[36]
Rt. Hon. F. J. Robinson, M.P.[37]	Rev. Andrew Thomson, Edinb.[38]
Henry Brougham, Esq. M.P.[39]	Professor Leslie, Edinburgh.[40]
Alexander Baring, Esq. M.P.[41]	Francis Jeffrey, Esq. Edinburgh.[42]

IN FRANCE

Marquis La Fayette.[43]	Duke de Rochefoucalt Laincourt.[44]
Sir Charles Stewart, Paris.[45]	

IN THE BRITISH COLONIES

The Earl of Dalhousie.[46]	Nor can we deny ourselves the
Sir Peregrine Maitland, K.C.B.[47]	pleasure of inserting in this list
Sir James Kempt, G.C.B.[48]	of free papers the name of our
Sir Thomas Brisbane, N. S. Wales.[49]	Statistical writer and exiled patriot
Jas. Stuart, Esq. of L.C. now in London.[50]	Robert Gourlay, London.[51]

IN THE UNITED STATES

The President.[52]	Wm. H. Crawford, Esq.[53]
Hon. De Witt Clinton.[54]	Daniel Webster, Esq.[55]

The Vice President.[56]   John Randolph, Esq.[57]
John Quincy Adams, Esq.[58]   Morris Birkbeck, Esq. Illinois.[59]
Henry Clay, Esq.[60]

So proud was the editor of this catalogue of prominent persons, he reprinted it in each of the next two issues. A rival editor soon mocked Mackenzie for sending free papers all the way to Australia! He was also taunted for not including on his free list Andrew Jackson, the War of 1812 "murderer" who "has a fair chance of succeeding to the Presidency of the land of Democrats and confused politics."[61]

These thirty-one important individuals might get the paper free, but the publisher made it clear that everyone else was expected to pay. The price was 6 pence an issue, £1.5s per annum – "if sent by mail the postage is charged." In his fourth issue he announced "We will receive payment in cash or produce, nay even old rags."[62] (Newspapers on both sides of the border commonly advertised their need for money and their willingness to accept payment in goods instead of cash.[63]) Unlike other purely local papers, one problem Mackenzie faced with his sending so many papers through the mail was postage. Regulations required that postages be paid quarterly in advance, at the rate of 4s per annum. American postal fees for newspapers were, he complained, more lenient.[64]

The paper listed subscription agents in some twenty-nine communities in Upper Canada, eight more in Lower Canada, four in the United States, and five in Great Britain. If, before putting out the *Colonial Advocate*, Mackenzie was politically unknown, he had nonetheless managed to weave an extensive network of connections.

As he began his editorial career, Mackenzie revealed something of his initial political naïveté. He assumed that all who were genuinely interested in Upper Canada, regardless of their political persuasion, would value his opinions and would pay to receive his paper. In the hope that they would subscribe, he informed his readers that he was sending some nine hundred copies of his first four issues free to "those persons, in this and the other British Colonies, whom we have judged to be most likely, from their situation and pursuits, to be…supporters." He had not selected them, he said, for their known political opinions. He recognized that many of them might "generally support the measures of the Provincial governments" (which he soon made clear that he did not). Indeed, he acknowledged that "not a few are members of, have places under, or enjoy pensions from, those governments." Nevertheless, he solicited their subscriptions to a periodical in which he "intended to discuss the merits of public men and public measures, with a freedom and plainness rather unusual in the greater part of our colonial publications."

Just how many of those nine hundred original recipients of free copies of the *Advocate* did in fact subscribe, is not known. What is clear is that the paper initially attracted enough attention and earned enough revenue to enable Mackenzie to continue it.

The paper's editor and publisher was also its main author. A portion of the content of each issue he copied from other papers – editors freely exchanged newspaper subscriptions for just that purpose – but he wrote most of the rest of it. He accepted submissions from others, but he did not encourage them, especially any which might cost him money. Indeed, he was scathing in his criticism of the poor quality of unsolicited material:

> Such of our friends as design to favour us with communications, will be pleased to pay the postage. Two thirds of the sonnets, songs, poems, canal-bubble-tales, air castle projects, puffs, political prophecies and animadversions on public & private characters, by Julias, Juniuses, Philos, Constant readers, and a host of other idle and useless names, usually intruded upon editors, are too dear in the reading; and the hardship is doubled when we have to send to the post office and pay for them.

He did, of course, welcome insertions of a commercial kind: "The extensive circulation of this paper will make it an object to persons advertising." So as not to detract from the editorial content of the paper, ads would not "be inserted in the body of this work, but…printed on the cover of each number." There would be no free repetitions: "Persons sending advertisements…will be pleased to state particularly how long they wish them continued; otherwise…they will be only once inserted." Some ads, however, which "like that of the Marmora Iron Works,[65] are of general interest," would be given "a few insertions gratis."

The Several Faces of William Lyon Mackenzie

The Queenston numbers of the *Colonial Advocate* set the pattern for Mackenzie's future as a journalist and as a politician. They also suggest something of the paradoxical nature of his personality. He had the heart of an idealist whose dreams were of an agrarian utopia, yet he had the head of a merchant whose values were very middle class. He questioned the judgment of persons in authority, yet he envied their influence. He was personally deeply religious, but he abhorred established religion. He admired American democratic ideals and practices, yet he cherished his

British, especially his Scottish heritage. He was a populist speaking to and for the ordinary people, yet he sprinkled his writing with erudite quotations, French and Latin phrases, and obscure historical and literary references.

Most of the first issue of the *Advocate* was devoted to a long rambling commentary reflecting on the state of Upper Canada and presenting future plans for the newspaper. The essay was both a prospectus for the new publication and a summary of the unknown editor's political ideas. As Mackenzie outlined his intentions, he also revealed the complexity of his character. He presented himself to his readers, as we have seen, as an entrepreneur, a merchant marketing his product. He was a publisher, promoting himself and his journal in businesslike ways, soliciting paid subscriptions from all who valued his product.

He was a knowledgeable editor. He knew how to read as well as write, and he had a phenomenal ability to recall what he had read. His first essay was sprinkled with quotations and allusions – at least fifty different literary, historical and biblical personages are referred to – in addition to his comments about contemporary political personalities. Poets, preachers, philosophers, jurists and statesmen all provided grist for his editorial mill.

He was also a reporter. From its earliest issues on, the columns of the *Advocate* included Mackenzie's own reports of court trials he observed, church services he visited, meetings he attended, events he witnessed, and stories he heard. He covered not only what happened in the Niagara area where he lived, he often travelled to other parts of the province (and later, into the United States) to give his readers first-hand reports and personal impressions.

He was also a news editor, informing his readers of current events around the world. By exchanging papers with editors in Canada, the United States and Britain, Mackenzie was soon receiving more than a hundred newspapers a week. He read them all and clipped from them – some items were copied in the *Advocate* immediately, others were saved for future use. He also kept up a constant correspondence with friends on both sides of the Atlantic and their letters were a source of news. In time he developed an exhaustive filing system for his many notes and clippings. (Thousands of these files are today carefully preserved in the Archives of Ontario.)[66]

He also saw himself as a teacher. He wanted the *Advocate* to provide useful information and practical advice to improve the lot of its yeomen readers – the subtitle said so: *Journal of Agriculture, Manufactures &*

Commerce. Somewhat naively perhaps, he saw himself as the expert, as the instructor of others.

Mackenzie may have been short on the experience needed to produce a newspaper, but he was long on the essentials of the editorial enterprise: memory, energy, attention to detail, love of language, egotistical self-confidence, and passion. He cared deeply about every matter that came within his ken. He wrote vigorously (sometimes viciously) about whatever subject was at hand.

But most of all, he was an independent commentator, a critic of the political establishment. He soon discovered that, much as he might wish to be an educator, he was destined to be an agitator; his political ideas were too incendiary. His paper attracted immediate attention – for his opinions much more than for his information

Agricultural and Economic Content

Mackenzie wanted his paper to be practical as well as political. "Agriculture" was to be his special interest – "the main cause of whatever portion of wealth we possess." Forthcoming issues would "devote a considerable space…to this useful art."

> We intend, according as we have room, to copy into the "Advocate" articles [newspaper editors all freely reprinted each other's articles] on Roads and Bridges, Townships, Diseases, Scotch emigrants, Irish ditto, English ditto, American ditto, Sheep, Cattle, Agricultural Societies, Wheat, Barley, Oats, Corn, Buck Wheat, Potatoes, etc. We will likewise give some account of the following articles and others, which may be termed properly articles of commerce: such as Flax, Hemp, Pot and Pearl Ashes, Bees' Wax, Honey, Lumber, Tobacco, Ginseng, etc. We have prepared for publication notices on Gypsum, Lime and manures, and we will occasionally touch upon the attendant science of horticulture.

With some prescience (the Niagara region where he lived is today known for its wineries), certainly with much presumption, he continued:

> Hops, and Grapes, the one very essential to the national British beverage of beer, the other the material from which we have wine, are articles requiring a degree of care and watchfulness beyond the means of common farmers.—But of even these we do not despair.—We will investigate the subject.

Not that Mackenzie had personal experience with any of this. He was a city boy. His birthplace, Dundee, had a population of 30,000. His father was a weaver, his apprenticeship was as an apothecary, his experience was as an accountant and a shopkeeper. He had never plowed a field, milked a cow or chopped down a tree in his life.

In addition to such agricultural subjects, there were matters of practical economy about which the editor intended to impart his expertise:

> A few of the articles connected with manufactures and inland and foreign commerce, of which it is our intention to speak, or upon which we have received essays: Foreign Trade.—British—other parts of Europe—Beyond the cape of Good Hope (including the tea monopoly)—With the W. Indies and Spanish Main—to South America—to the United States— Fur Trade—Whale fishery—Codfishing—Exchanges—Bounties and Drawbacks—Excise Duties and Customs, &c. &c. Here is a wide field for speculation….
>
> On the subject of manufactures and trades we have prepared essays on the paper, iron, hat, linen, cotton, woolen, maple sugar, potash, hemp, cordage, and salt manufactures—also on Distilling, Brewing, Weaving, dyeing, printing, bookselling, tanning, ship-building, and on Flour-mills, and Glassworks; these and notices of other arts will be inserted successively as the limits of the publication will admit.

There is nothing in his life to suggest that he had special expertise in any of these matters. But his travels and experience in Canada had convinced him that there was a crying need for such knowledge. He thought, through his paper, he could provide it.

One subject Mackenzie wrote about again and again was canal construction – a matter he knew something about. He had worked for canal companies in England and at Lachine in Lower Canada. In 1824, as work progressed on the Erie canal – designed to link New York City with Lake Erie and the whole Great Lakes system – there were a number of Canadian proposals for canals. (There were, as yet, no railways – rivers, lakes and connecting canals were the paths of transportation.) The *Advocate* reported on several of them. (Mackenzie would retain this interest in canals for many years, often to the distress of those in the political establishment.)

Newspapers in Upper Canada

When, in May of 1824, Mackenzie started down the road of a career as an independent journalist in Upper Canada, it was a path already well trod. The *Colonial Advocate* was not the first independent paper in the province.

The first newspaper was *The Upper Canada Gazette*, the official government journal initiated in 1793 in Newark (now Niagara-on-the-Lake), the temporary capital of Upper Canada. From its first issue, the Gazette demonstrated that newspaper publishing was a political activity. The *Gazette* had been created to be an instrument for the propagation of government policies and programmes. Its first editor printer, Louis Roy, lasted less than two years in his post. He was let go for reasons of ill health, and for suspicions of democratic tendencies. All of the succeeding *Gazette* editors would be subject to intense political scrutiny. Most of them had trouble living up to the expectations of their government employers.

The second editor of the *Gazette*, Gideon Tiffany, along his brother Sylvester, had been lured from New York state to take over the paper, there being no qualified printer available in Canada. Gideon was soon criticized for his pro-Yankee sympathies, and, worse, he was convicted of blasphemy, fined, jailed and forced to resign. Later *Gazette* editors were less harshly treated, but nearly all of them found themselves subject to sharp criticism from their government – their average length of tenure was less than four years.[67]

In the first *Advocate*, Mackenzie delighted in quoting the parting comment of the most recent editor of the *Gazette*, Dr. Robert Horne.[68] He resigned as editor because he was "thoroughly disgusted with a situation always peculiarly anxious and disagreeable."

If serving as the King's printer in Upper Canada was difficult, operating a newspaper without government support was even more hazardous.

The Tiffany brothers were the first to try. When the official *Gazette* moved with the government to the new provincial capital of York late in 1796, the Niagara peninsula was left with no newspaper. In 1798 the Tiffanys moved into the vacuum and started the *Canada Constellation*, the first independent newspaper in Upper Canada. It died a year or so later. Sylvester Tiffany tried again in 1801 with the *Niagara Herald*, but with no better success. These papers were independent, but they were singularly uncritical of government policies. Quite the contrary, they regularly contained expressions of praise and satisfaction for conditions in Upper Canada. Nonetheless, simply by printing more American news than English news, the editors aroused the distrust and even the ire of colonial officials, even though most readers, whether loyalists or not, were immigrants from the United States who still had connections there. At one point Sylvester Tiffany was threatened with some unstated accusations of "treasonable or seditious conduct," although he was never brought to trial. By 1803 Gideon Tiffany had moved on to other pursuits and Sylvester had moved back to New York state.[69]

The next independent paper in the province, the *Upper Canada Guardian*, was also published in Niagara. It was the work of Joseph Willcocks, a former officeholder who had fallen out with the government, but who was nevertheless elected to the Assembly. His paper has been called the province's first "opposition newspaper," but so few copies are extant (it was published for about five years) that it is difficult to judge its content. Willcocks, however, was indeed a sharp critic of the government. His disenchantment became so complete that in the middle of the War of 1812 he switched sides and joined the Americans, only to be killed in battle shortly before that war ended.[70]

The Niagara region was a seedbed of editorial discontent. Soon after the war the *Niagara Spectator* was born. It died in 1819 when its editor, Bartemas Ferguson, was convicted of publishing sedition – he had printed attacks on the government in articles by Robert Gourlay written from the Niagara jail.[71]

Independent journalism did somewhat better in Kingston. The first paper printed there, in 1810, was the *Kingston Gazette* (after 1819, the *Chronicle and Gazette*). It was still going strong when Mackenzie began his editorial enterprise. The secret of journalistic success in Kingston was to be ardently loyal so that the paper would receive government support through official advertising. A more liberal Kingston paper, the *Upper Canada Herald*, started up in competition in 1819 and was able to survive without significant government advertising, but it was never particularly hostile to the government in its editorial content.

In York, John Carey began an independent paper in 1820. (Unfortunately very few copies of it exist, even though it was published weekly for more than ten years). Carey was mainly concerned with York and Home District matters, rather than (like Mackenzie) publishing for the whole province. Similarly, Andrew Heron began the *Gleaner* in Niagara in 1818 with a view to serving the area and with few political axes to grind.

Thus, when the *Colonial Advocate* was born, there were only six other newspapers in all of Upper Canada – two in York, two in Kingston, one in Niagara, and one, the *Recorder* in Brockville, which began in 1821.[72]

(By the time of the Rebellion, there were some thirty newspapers being published in the province, but sixty or more had come and gone in the meantime.)[73]

Political Context

How in 1824 Mackenzie caught the political bug and what prompted him to start a newspaper is not entirely clear. The obvious immediate reason was elections for the Parliament of Upper Canada set for that summer.

During the four years he had been in Canada, Mackenzie had traveled widely, had formed many friendships and had made contacts everywhere. Not a candidate himself (that would come not come until 1828), Mackenzie nevertheless showed no hesitation in plunging into the political waters. The *Advocate* was his first splash.

Issue number nine of the *Advocate* was three weeks late. The editor had gone off on a trip through part of the province. The election campaigns had begun to heat up around the province and he wanted to report on them first hand. In his travels he met many candidates face to face and often spoke publicly at political rallies. But his reports were more than political commentary, they were a traveller's sharing of his observations and experiences. (In the course of the next few years Mackenzie travelled, he later claimed, a hundred thousand miles in the Canadas and the northern United States,[74] and wrote about his journeys, often under the pseudonym of Peter Russell.)

After his return the editor recognized that not everyone would be happy with his published views "respecting the merits of many of the candidates." Some readers might cancel their subscriptions:

> Let them withdraw their names — surely I care not — if the public
> cannot support an independent press, it is but giving up the paper at
> last, and I would rather do that than withhold praise or blame where I
> consider it merited…. If my brother editors choose to pursue what they
> conceive to be a safer course, namely, to make no remarks on the merits
> or demerits of individuals, I find no fault but only act up to my sense of
> right, as a public journalist, and confessing my liability to err, shall never
> feel above owning myself in the wrong in opinion where I am satisfied
> beyond proof that I have been in error.[75]

The danger of losing financial support was very real. Throughout his publishing career Mackenzie was often plagued by money problems. His large circulation might attract advertisers, but there were not enough paying subscribers to meet his printing and postage costs. (It would be a number of years before he was able to combine political popularity with financial stability – for a time in the 1830s.)

At this stage in his political development – indeed throughout his life, except for the few months prior to the 1837 Rebellion – Mackenzie had faith in the electoral process. He believed that electing reform candidates to Parliament could alter the course of government. He wanted his farmer readers to use their votes. He might well have been quoting one of his own speeches when he urged on his readers:

> Up then, and be doing. Stir yourselves, like men, and strike at the roots of corruption, in the person of our late corrupt representatives. Send them to beg for the crumbs that fall from Sir Peregrine's table, and never again trust your religion, your fortunes, your power of mind, and indeed all you can or ought to be…[to those] worthless beings who have no claim to your favour unless it be on account of their having made a low bow or given you a friendly shake of the hand previous to an election.[76]

Politically, Upper Canada in the 1820s was relatively stable. Created in 1791 – separated from Lower Canada (Quebec) as a haven for Loyalists from the American Revolution – the new province had grown (mostly through immigration from the United States) to a population of 150,000.[77] It had come through early difficulties and, more importantly, the stresses of the War of 1812. By the spring of 1824, Lieutenant-Governor Sir Peregrine Maitland had been in office for nearly six years – his administration had been marked by some controversy, but nothing to cause it serious problems. The general economy was comparatively prosperous, although Mackenzie, among others, did not see it that way.

Upper Canada, according to Mackenzie, was not the place of progress and prosperity that it could be, that it ought to be. In full agreement, he quoted, the "woeful intelligence" once expressed by Charles Fothergill, editor of the official *Upper Canada Gazette*:

> This fine country has so long languished in a state of comparative stupor and inactivity, whilst our more enterprising neighbours are laughing us to scorn.

(That same year, 1824, E.G. Stanley, a British aristocrat who would later become British Prime Minister, toured North America. In his personal journal he noted "the universal energy and activity which pervades" the United States, comparing it to "the general supineness and listlessness in which [Canada] appears to be sunk." But he never said so publicly![78])

In Mackenzie's mind, there was no question as to where the responsibility for this dismal state of affairs lay. His first *Advocate* editorial began with an evaluation of the province's chief administrator. Lieutenant-Governor Maitland was teasingly described as

a knight of noble birth & noble connexions, who, after spending his
earlier days amidst the din of war and the turmoil of camps, has gained
enough renown in Europe to enable him to enjoy himself, like the country
he governs, in inactivity — whose migrations are by water, from York to
Queenston, and from Queenston to York, who knows our wants as he
gains a knowledge of the time of day, by report; in one case by the report
of the Niagara gun; in the other, by the Gazette.

There was more than teasing to Mackenzie's discontent, however.
He used his pen to prod Maitland by commenting:

For the present we cannot remember any thing he has done of a public
nature worth recording. As a private gentleman, as a human and an
amiable man, as a Christian we respect him. We wish we could say as
much of him as a governor. But what can we say? What road has he
made? What Canal has been begun in his time? Of what agricultural
society is he the patron, president or benefactor? What does the domestic
manufactures of the Province owe him?

Such a passive governor was, by Mackenzie's good Scottish measure,
not only worthless, but, in "his enjoyment of a princely salary," expensive.
In contrast to Maitland, readers were called to

look at DeWitt Clinton [the governor of New York state]…wasting the
best years of his life in improving the resources of his country without
fee or reward, other than the self approbation of his own mind, and the
applause of millions of his fellow citizens.

When Fothergill read these words, he promptly accused the new
journalist of promoting "democracy, disloyalty and foul-play."[79] Mackenzie
had violated the first Canadian commandment: Thou shalt never
unfavourably compare this country with the United States!

Despite his hostility to Maitland, Mackenzie did not initially attack all
colonial authority. Of the Earl of Dalhousie, the governor-in-chief of all
of British North America (thus the man above Maitland) the editor
had this to say:

We are far from saying, or even thinking, that the nobleman now at the
head of the Colonial Government in North America, is other than an able
and a prudent ruler. It is the system we condemn. Lord Dalhousie we
believe to be a humane, well designing and amiable aristocrat. We respect
him for his moderation and good temper.

Such expressions of goodwill toward the ruling nobility, however,
did not prevent the new editor from continuing on with his catalogue
of political grievances.

Religion and the Clergy Reserves

One contentious issue of the day (and for many days to come) was the use of the so-called "clergy reserves." When Upper Canada was created in 1791, one-seventh of all land was set aside to provide support for "a Protestant clergy." As officially interpreted, this meant exclusively the clergy of the Church of England.[80]

Mackenzie made no bones about his own religious convictions:

It may not be amiss for us here to state, that we are Calvinists, and profess to believe the Westminster confession of faith as now adopted by the church in the northern part of our native island of Great Britain.

He did not, at this early stage in his editorial and political career, advocate the separation of church and state. He wanted financial support for all faiths, at least, all Christian faiths. But he did not believe in an established church. In Canada, the Church of England should not receive special benefits.

We can state, from personal knowledge of both countries, that Canada is much worse off for religious instruction than are the United States.... We are in a state something like Ireland; a priesthood who do nothing, consume all, and the working clergy suffer thereby.

Mackenzie approved of the original idea of the Clergy Reserves, but not the interpretation.

In no part of the constitution of the Canadas, is the wisdom of the British legislature more apparent, than its setting apart a portion of this country, while it yet remained a wilderness, for the support of religion.... One seventh of our time only, is required by the divine command, to be devoted to the particular service of Jehovah, and here the profit or income of only a like proportion of our country is to be employed in the support of religion.— So far well.

However,

the Canadas are peopled by emigrants from many countries…they have been accustomed to enjoy many different religious opinions and forms of worship, or have perhaps left their respective countries that they might be enabled here peaceably to worship their maker according to their consciences…. The imperial parliament did not consult the best interests of the people nor of Britain, when it endowed the professors of one faith, with the rents and emoluments of the lands…thereby establishing in the nineteenth century, a militant dominant church.

For the Clergy Reserve income to be given exclusively to the Church of England was wrong!

> 1st. Because the persons dissenting from the church of England, being then & now more than nine-tenths of the population, are thereby persecuted....
>
> 2nd. Because, this church, so established, and being in possession of territories which will...yield an immense revenue, may very greatly endanger our liberties, by the temporal influence it will thereby acquire...
>
> 3rd. Because distrust, discontent, and dissentions are engendered by this division of funds set apart for the support of religion....

There was another reason, one that especially irked Mackenzie:

> 4th. Because this seventh, if given to support only one class of Christians, is equivalent to a system of temporal rewards and punishments; and if this is resorted to as a means of establishing religious opinions, it will make hypocrites enough. We have known ministers connected with other churches, in coming into this province, change their religion and become Episcopal clergymen. Christian charity induces us to believe that their motives were disinterested, but as some of them have grown very bigoted to their adopted faith, many attributing the change of principle thus miraculously achieved to far less honorable motives than either conviction or conversion.

Although unnamed, the reference to ministers who "change their religion" was to the Rev. Dr. John Strachan, rector of the church at York (soon to become Archdeacon and later Bishop). In 1799, when he first came to Canada to serve as a teacher in Kingston, Strachan was a Presbyterian. In 1803 he converted to the Church of England, was ordained to its ministry and appointed to serve the church in Cornwall. He moved to York in 1812 and began a rapid rise in power and influence. In 1815 he was appointed to the Executive Council of the Province and in 1820 to the Legislative Council. All his life Strachan was a vigourous promoter of an established church.[81] (Attacking Strachan became for Mackenzie almost an obsession. Throughout his entire career as a journalist, virtually every issue of every newspaper Mackenzie published made some direct or indirect reference to Strachan.)

To Mackenzie, the answer to the Clergy Reserves question was clear. Use the income to promote all Christian religions. Give each one its share.

> We are clearly of opinion that Catholic and Protestant, Episcopalian and Presbyterian, Methodist and Baptist, Quaker and Tunker, deserve a share

alike in the income produced by these lands; and we trust we shall yet see a law enacted by which the ministers of every body of professing Christians, being British subjects, shall receive equal benefits from these clergy reserves; for we conceive it would remove a grievance which, if suffered to remain, may be the means of much evil—and indeed may be the cause of greater injury to British interests here than we chose to anticipate.

(His prediction was correct – disputes over the Clergy Reserves continued to plague the province for many years. Mackenzie, however, changed his mind on the matter. Along with most other reformers, he soon was advocating that the Reserves be abolished altogether and that the money be used instead for general purposes such as schools and roads. The Reserves controversy became one of the grievances which led to the 1837 Rebellion. Not until 1854 was the question finally settled.)

Education

Another subject of importance in the young province was education. Mackenzie, as he waxed eloquently to declare, was for it:

> Arts and sciences, manufactures and commerce, have greatly progressed
> thro'out Europe and America during the last fifty years. The invention of
> the steam engine, and the useful application of steam pressure, has placed
> us centuries in advance of even the last generation, in point of power.…
> Let us, therefore, lose no time, but free from party spirit and narrow
> sectarian motives in our institutions, endeavor to benefit by the general
> diffusion of knowledge. We ought to enrich the minds of our youth, by
> giving them such instruction and conformation of character as may
> enable them to serve their country, by the practical application of a
> systematic education, and like William Pitt,[82] to blend the wisdom of
> age, with the complexion of youth.

Scot that he was, the writer was not satisfied with the present, inadequate system:

> The education which a boy now receives at any of the district schools is
> very costly.… Far more—aye, more than double what would be required
> in Scotland.

Mackenzie initially told his readers he planned in future issues to devote space to the topic of education. (Indeed, the quality and availability of public education would be a constant source of dissatisfaction among reformers in Upper Canada.) The editor himself was about to become a trustee of the local Queenston school (as he reported in his third issue).[83] He had given the matter much thought:

> We would wish to impress on the minds of every one of our readers, the truth of this important quotation from Addison: "I consider a human soul without education like marble in the quarry, which shews none of its inherent beauties, until the skill of the polisher fetches out the colours."[84]

One educational matter much in discussion at this time in Upper Canada was the possible creation of a university in Upper Canada. Mackenzie quoted Strachan, who had been promoting the idea:

> The liberal professions now demand the establishment of a university.... Young men designed for the bar, have not the necessary opportunities for preparing themselves for that important profession. The students of medicine, the sons of liberal merchants and of the more opulent landholders, would certainly attend a seminary on an extensive scale; and it is very certain that, in a few years after its establishment, more than one hundred students would be found at the university of Upper Canada.[85]

Mackenzie favoured the idea (even if it was Strachan's), but with reservations:

> If it is to be an arm of our hierarchy; if students are to be tied down by tests and oaths, to support particular dogmas, as is the case in Oxford, the institution will have no good purpose.

No matter what his specific subject, the outspoken journalist could never resist taking swipes at the ruling élite (later to be dubbed the "Family Compact"). A university was needed because it would broaden the power base in the province:

> We very much want men in Canada who have received a liberal education; men untainted by the enjoyment of power and place, who, if called on, would not hesitate to sacrifice their personal interests for the good of their country....
>
> We want barristers who would at all times prefer, on principle, to plead the cause of a poor man oppressed, rather than of a rich oppressor; who would rather physic pomp than pamper it; rather despise arrogance... than cringe to and flatter it.
>
> We want churchmen who would come up to, or nearly to the picture of a gospel minister...lovers more of the flock, than of the fleece.

Mackenzie held great hopes for the future of the Upper Canada. The progress of the province, he believed, would be determined by the independence of mind of those who assumed its leadership:

If we desire to see in the pulpits and in the ranks, at the bar and on the bench, in the senate and in the field, in the counting-house and in the navy, our Canadian Blairs[86] and Fenelons;[87] our Erskines[88] and Romillys;[89] our Pitts,[90] Foxes,[91] Cannings,[92] and Clintons;[93] our Moores[94] and Washingtons;[95] our Nelsons[96] and Duncans;[97] our Burkes[98] and Sheridans,[99] and Broughams[100] and Barings;[101] if we desire, hope and expect British America to produce men eminent both at home and abroad; if, in fact, we entertain a single wish for the welfare of our country, we must encourage — liberally encourage — competent professors of science and literature to emigrate hither.

Constitutional Reform

Much that was wrong with Upper Canada could be put right, Mackenzie believed, if the province had greater control of its own political destiny. He sought to loosen, but not untie, the colonial bonds:

> Good conduct deserves reward, not punishment; and it is not surely too great a boon to ask, that Canada, as the reward of her obedience should be allowed a little more freedom of action, and be less subject to a distant parental control.

(The exact nature of the changes Mackenzie wanted he did not spell out – probably he had not thought them through. Certainly, at this stage in his thinking, there is no clear advocacy of "responsible government" as it would eventually evolve in Canada, that is, the executive branch of government responsible and accountable to the elected Assembly. Later generations would sometimes portray Mackenzie as an early advocate of responsible government, but there is little in his first *Advocate* editorials to support that view.)

In Mackenzie's opinion, the parliamentary system was not functioning properly. Look at the Assembly:

> Our elected men…unfortunately, are so attached to pensions, powers, places, titles, honours and emoluments, that the simple Farmer we sent four years ago to York to guard our interests, returns among us so bedizened with honors, justice-ships, collector-ships, commissioner-ships, majorities and colonelcies, that we scarcely know the Tom Hedge, our neighbour; and he, on his part, is so familiar with the little great as scarcely to condescend to remember us.

And the appointed Legislative Council was even worse:

> Have the members of our Legislative Councils ever been other than the most obsequious, cringing worshippers of power? Have the honourables

and reverends and right reverends ever attempted ought towards
consolidating your liberties? Have they not, on the other hand, done
all that in them lay to abridge, to curtail, aye, to crush them?

The province of Upper Canada, as envisaged by the first Lieutenant-
Governor, John Graves Simcoe, was "singularly blest" with a constitution
which is "the very image and transcript of that of Great Britain."[102] The
Legislative Council was to be something similar to the House of Lords.
Mackenzie scoffed at the idea:

> Where, where is the resemblance? Not in their mode of election, surely,
> for they of Canada are only for life…and are almost always selected from
> the servile tools of power, while the British Aristocracy represents a very
> considerable proportion of the wealth and dignity of an ancient
> monarchy, and are independent both of the crown and of the people.…
> And many of them…have often, and not in vain, maintained with their
> estates and with their lives the liberties of Britain in her day of danger.

This reference in deference to the authority of the British House of
Lords was but an aside, however. For Mackenzie, the ultimate political
authority was the people (albeit, like nearly all the reformers of his time,
this meant males over twenty-one who owned land or other property).
The first *Advocate* jeremiad of discontents concluded on an up note.
From its style and cadences, one might think the editor was on a stump
addressing a crowd:

> To yourselves, therefore, Farmers, in the hour of your trial, must you look
> for aid. The eyes of the whole of the Colonies, and of America, are fixed
> on you. You are the only true nobility that this country can boast of.
> Through you only, by your Representatives, can the real state of things
> become known in the British senate. If ye choose the wisest, the honestest,
> the most esteemed of your body; men who have been long known as
> tried patriots, in whose souls the voice of freedom is not yet extinct; who
> hold no offices under, or receive any gifts from the Crown; and who, as
> fathers, as husbands, as members of society, are kind and brotherly minded;
> men of cultivated minds and discreet demeanour, fearing God and hating
> covetousness.[103] If to such as these ye trust your liberties, there is yet hope
> for your country, that such representatives will assert your rights, recover
> your due influence, and be a means to consolidate your freedom. But if ye
> will, as heretofore, choose collectors and king's advocates, ambassadors,
> parasites and sycophants, to manage your affairs, you will dearly rue it; you
> and the generations that shall be hereafter. Look at Spain—Look at
> Greece—Look at Revolutionary France—behold the sad effects of

misgovernment and beware!—The errors were in the princes in the end,
but sprang from an effeminacy in the people in the beginning.

He closed with a reference to the reformers of Lower Canada who
for years had been embroiled in struggles with the Colonial government:

> The brave stand which a majority of the Lower Canada members of
> Assembly have at all times made against the encroachments of arbitrary
> power, is creditable to them, and will yet be beneficial to their constituents;
> sooner or later they will succeed; and in the end they will obtain their claims.

Stop Press

Mackenzie printed this essay, two columns wide on white paper, as a sixteen page octavo booklet with a pale blue four-page wrap-around cover
devoted largely to advertising.[104] At the last minute, however, the cover
copy was scrapped to make room for a report of a jury inquiry into the
death of the area's most prominent citizen, Colonel Robert Nichol,
MP:[105]

> The awful and sudden end of this unfortunate gentleman, discloses
> circumstances so full of general interest, so deeply and powerfully
> expressive of the feeble tenure by which the living hold possession of
> their clay tenements, that we have thought to devote a few of our pages
> to give an account of so deplorable an event.

Nichol had died under suspicious circumstances. As he was riding
home at night in a storm, his horse had gone off the path, slipped, and
Nichol had been thrown several hundred feet down the steep precipice
of a bank of the Niagara river. Mackenzie described the scene:

> It is a dreadful place, some 60 or 70 feet above the margin of the river.
> Pieces of his skull and brains and much blood were observed on the spot
> where he had fallen … the very place where not he only, but also many
> Americans had years before, at the battle of Queenston, found a grave.

After summarizing the testimony of various people before the jury,
the report continued:

> The jury seeing no cause to believe otherwise, returned a verdict of
> ACCIDENTAL DEATH. By the evidence produced they could not have done
> otherwise.

To make room in the paper for this report, paid advertising was omitted.
The publisher sacrificed private income for public information – and
personal publicity. Mackenzie himself had been foreman of the jury.

(Mackenzie could never be content with being a disinterested independent commentator; he could never remain aloof. He was always a participant, always caught up in whatever events or issues were of immediate interest. However adept he was as a businessman, as at times he surely was, he would often sacrifice profits to proclaim his principles.)

Despite his own jury's finding in regard to Nichol's death, the editor remained suspicious that the death might have been the work of some secret enemy.

> There is a mystery about this man's death that we cannot unravel. It is
> hard to suppose that any one could have been so barbarous as on that
> stormy and dreadful night to have forced him into certain destruction;
> yet it is really marvellous how he, with a steady horse, which so well knew
> the way, should have missed the path.

(Mackenzie could never remain content when doubts persisted. There was always a deeply skeptical streak to his personality.)

Accusations of Disloyalty

The *Advocate* quickly caught the attention of readers throughout Upper Canada, to the dismay of some and the delight of others.

Mackenzie soon found himself at odds with Charles Fothergill, editor of the *Upper Canada Gazette*. As we have seen, Mackenzie had quoted Fothergill's complaint that: "this fine country has so long languished in a state of comparative stupor and inactivity, whilst our more enterprising neighbours are laughing us to scorn." Fothergill hotly responded that he had been quoted out of context and regretted that he had to stoop "to brush away any little dirt that may be squirted upon our garments." He condescendingly dismissed Mackenzie, suggesting that the "smallness of the offender" made him hardly worth answering.[106]

Nonetheless Fothergill proceeded to reveal the depth of his irritation by devoting five columns in his next two issues to pouring scorn on the impertinent *Advocate* editor. The new paper was denounced as:

> the most insolent and wretched specimen of a total abandonment of all
> truth, principle, sense and decorum — we have ever witnessed — Its
> very extravagance, however, will prove its own antidote; and even as the
> scorpion, when surrounded by a wall of fire, is said to retire into the
> centre of its own narrow circle, and there commit a *felo de se* by the
> sting of its own tail, so will the venom of this malignant libeller, of
> genuine and unaffected worth, recoil on his recreant head.[107]

Before long Mackenzie was also embroiled in argument with other editors: John Carey of the *Observer*, Andrew Heron of the *Gleaner*, James Macfarlane of the *Chronicle*.

To make matters worse, in his first issue Mackenzie favourably quoted "a very honest man…a sincere well wisher of the country," Robert Gourlay. Gourlay had been banished from the province for seditious activity in 1819. Mackenzie did not arrive in Upper Canada until the next year. Nonetheless, he understood that association with Gourlay was politically dangerous. The new editor firmly stated that he was no Gourlayite.

Attorney General John Beverley Robinson, however, was not dissuaded by this disclaimer. The day after the *Advocate* appeared, Robinson wrote privately to a friend, "Another reptile of the Gourlay species has sprung up…a conceited red-headed fellow with an apron. He publishes a weekly pamphlet and has begun *secundum artem* by attacking the Lt. Governor.…What vermin!"[108]

Although Robinson was barely mentioned in the first *Advocate*, Mackenzie had little use for him. Some four-and-a-half columns in the third number of the paper were devoted to an attack on the Attorney General for his extravagance and disservice to Upper Canada while on an official trip to England the previous year.[109]

(For the next decade and more, Robinson would be second only to John Strachan as a target for Mackenzie's editorial arrows.)

In his first *Advocate*, as has been noted, Mackenzie clearly stated, "We like American liberty well, but greatly prefer British liberty." This unequivocal declaration of British loyalty was hardly sufficient, however. Opponents quickly spotted Mackenzie's admiration of Americans as his Achilles' heel. Any truth in his critique of Canadian policies and officials could be discounted by dismissing the author as disloyal.

Mackenzie was new to Upper Canada. He had no family connections with the United Empire Loyalist migrations following the American Revolution. He had not known the threat to Canadian sovereignty of the War of 1812. He had no personal experience of American economic competition. In 1824 he did not understand – and perhaps he never was to understand – how deep were the feelings of anti-Americanism in so many Canadians.

The editor quickly discovered that he could not disregard his critics' charges of disloyalty. When Fothergill accused him of "democracy, disloyalty and foul-play,"[110] Mackenzie's outraged response may have rallied some to his support, but it also must have hardened any opposition:

> The doctrines I have advocated will bear any inspection, for they are of a
> truly British stamp. "To be taxed without being represented, is contrary to
> the maxims of law and the constitution." [Lord Chatham] I have briefly
> adverted to the danger which British interests will be liable to suffer if this
> truth is disregarded, set at naught, and trampled on. — Is this democracy
> and foul play? Then am I indeed disloyal.
>
> I have said that I despise and hold in utter detestation the venal tribe,
> who stupid as the beasts that perish, are now fattening on the spoils of the
> country. — Is this sedition? Then am I seditious.
>
> I have pointed out the neglect which successive governors, more or
> less ignorant of our wants, have been guilty of in regard to domestic
> improvements, and have delivered my opinion with the freedom of a
> Briton, in Britain. Is this treason? Then I am also a rebellious subject.
>
> I have spoken well of the institutions and of the people of a neighbour-
> ing country, where I found either deserving of praise; and I have been
> equally free with my censures, where I conceived them merited. — Is
> this disaffection, calumny, and detraction? Then am I a calumniator, and
> a disaffected person.
>
> In short, when Mr. Fothergill can prove that black is white, and that
> white is black, that evil is good, and good evil — then will he also be able
> to hold a Mackenzie up to the world as an enemy to his country — but
> not till then.[111]

Mackenzie smarted under accusations of disloyalty. He cited his own
loyal pedigree. Both grandfathers had fought for Bonnie Prince Charlie
at Culloden (a fact hardly reassuring to readers loyal to King George).
His humble widowed mother had reared him through periods of poverty,
"never neglecting divine worship," though he later "became careless
and neglected public and private devotion"[112] (a confession hardly
enheartening to any who doubted him).

A correspondent to the *Niagara Gleaner* quickly scoffed at this defence
which,

> besides containing a genealogical account of the Editor's progenitors,
> furnishes a piece of information still more important to the Canadian
> public, namely, that the Editor himself, in the early part of his life, had
> but very little to eat. I am not at all disposed to doubt the veracity of his
> statement, as his appearance bears ample testimony.[113]

During the War of 1812, distrust of Americans became almost a paranoia
in Upper Canada. In the years following, Canadian authorities did all

they could to discourage American immigration and to reduce the status of anyone with American connections. The "Alien question," that is, the legal status of anyone originally from the United States, was a major political issue. Measures were proposed to deprive such settlers of voting rights, and even of property rights. The Conservative establishment found it very useful to dismiss every effort at reform as tainted by American influences.

Mackenzie, on the other hand, saw a prosperity across the river in New York clearly far exceeding anything in Upper Canada. The reasons for that superiority were to him obvious – Canadian colonial officials were self-satisfied and self-serving persons promoting only their own self-interests. Unlike their neighbours to the south, they had not taken advantage of opportunities for economic development, had not invested in roads and canals, had not bolstered local agriculture and manufacturing, had not promoted genuine self-government.

Mackenzie himself had little to fear from the United States. In his four years in Canada, he had come to know many American settlers. He admired their skills and their spirit. He found their opinions not unlike ideas he had absorbed in his native Dundee. To him such men were allies. In August he published in his paper a lengthy consideration of the question "Should citizens of the United States be encouraged and invited to settle in the Canadas?"[114] His answer was firmly affirmative.

Mackenzie argued that the real danger for those living in British North America (or Cabotia, as he was then apt to call it) came not from American influences but from administrative injustices. If changes could be made, there would be nothing to fear from the United States. The best answer to republicanism was reform – and he catalogued a long list of grievances over matters like land policies, patronage, election practices, religious favoritism, post office management, and tax revenues. Later in the summer of 1824 (after the elections were over and it was clear that the new Assembly was not likely to be much different from the last) Mackenzie called for a convention to redress these wrongs, to create a new constitution.[115] (It was a call he would repeat in 1837 as he rallied support for rebellion).

Not surprisingly, Andrew Heron quickly responded that Canadians were not about to model their constitution on the American. He advised Mackenzie

> to follow the example of that great Reformer, Mohomet — that when
> the mountain would not come to him, he went to the mountain. Since

> the good people of the United States cannot be induced to come here,
> unless we comply with some of the reforms or changes pointed out by
> the Editor, which it is strongly suspected we will not…the Editor had
> better go to them.[116]

On October, Mackenzie again felt compelled to assert that he did not
favour copying everything American. Indeed, he expressed his dismay in
no uncertain terms:

> I am afraid that…I have hitherto been disposed to think too well of
> the American government and to overlook some of the peculiar
> characteristicks which render it more beautiful in theory than virtuous
> in practice. Its…connexion with two millions of our fellow creatures
> by only one tie, that of the tyrant over the oppressed, the strong over
> the weak, the slave owner over the slave, grieves and distresses me. I have,
> of late, perused very carefully some of the leading journals of the
> Union…where I anticipated pleasure from learning the wise enactments
> of a virtuous community, I have been shocked with accounts of political
> fraud, bribery, and corruption.[117]

The Brock Monument

The fiery editor's first real controversy – and what first brought his
paper to public attention beyond Niagara – was an entirely unexpected
Brock monument episode.

In April the *Montreal Canadian Review* had carried a report from the
provincial capital:

> On Saturday, [the] 24th … his Excellency the Lieutenant-Governor,
> attended by his staff, was met by the Honourable Members of the
> Executive Council, the Judges of the Court of King's Bench, and the
> Gentlemen of the Bar, with the Magistrates, and principal inhabitants
> of York, in procession, for the purpose of laying the foundation stone of
> the new Gaol and Court House about to be erected in this Town. —
> A sovereign and half-sovereign of gold, and several coins of silver and
> copper, of the present Reign, together with some newspapers and other
> memorials of the present day, were deposited in a cavity of the stone, over
> which, a plate of copper, bearing an appropriate inscription, was placed;
> and after his Excellency had given the first blow, with a hammer handed
> to him for the purpose, the ceremony concluded with several hearty
> cheers for all who were present.[118]

There can be little doubt that this inspired the *Advocate* editor to copy the idea. At his instigation, on the first of June, with full Masonic rites (Mackenzie himself was not a Freemason), a ceremony was held to lay the foundation stone for a tower honouring Major-General Sir Isaac Brock, killed while repelling American invaders in 1812. A sealed bottle – containing a patriotic inscription, some old coins, a copy of the current *Upper Canada Gazette*, and a copy of the first *Colonial Advocate* – was placed (by Mackenzie) in a hollowed-out cavity in the foundation stone. The inscription (authored by Mackenzie) was printed up in the shape of a funeral urn:

The Foundation Stone

Of This Monument

Sacred to the memory

Of

Major General Sir ISAAC BROCK, Knight,

Was laid

the first day of June,

in the year of our Lord,

1824

Of the world

5928,

And of the reign of His Most Excellent Majesty

KING GEORGE IVth

His Excellency Lieutenant General George,

Earl of Dalhousie, Lord Ramsey, and

Baron Dalhousie of Dalhousie Castle,

Knight Grand Cross of the most

Honourable Military Order

Of the Bath, Governor,

Vice Admiral and Commander in Chief of the

Forces in and of

BRITISH NORTH AMERICA.

His Excellency

Major General Sir Peregrine Maitland,

Knight Commander of the most Hon-

ourable Military Order of the Bath,

Knight of the Russian Order of

St. George, and of William

in the Netherlands,

Lieutenant Governor
of the Province of Upper Canada,
and
Commander in Chief of the Forces therein.
The Right Reverend Jacob, Lord Bishop of
Quebec.
The Right Worshipful Simon M'Gillivray, Provincial Grand Master of the Grand Lodge
of Upper Canada.

Mortar was applied and the foundation stone was covered with another large stone so that the capsule would there remain "until some future generation, long after we and our contemporaries are forgotten, shall perhaps discover it hid amidst the wreck of ages."[119]

It did not rest there that long. When Sir Peregrine Maitland learned of all this, he was appalled. The Lieutenant-Governor was not about to allow a journal so critical of his administration to desecrate Brock's memorial − or to tarnish his own future reputation. He immediately ordered the capsule's removal. Although the monument had by then reached a considerable height, the masonry was taken down and the vessel disinterred. The commissioner in charge of the removal reportedly threw the bottle in the air and cried "so go all Mackenzie's enemies."[120]

The editor's name in Upper Canada was then and there made. This "premature resurrection," as Mackenzie delightedly dubbed the affair,[121] was the first of many incidents in his life when the excessive reaction of opponents worked to his political advantage. (This one certainly lost him no local prestige − a few months later, when Brock's body was interred in the monument, Mackenzie's press printed the day's formal schedule of events.[122])

Nor did the matter end there. In Ancaster a Free Church had just been formed. Not to be outdone by the Brock monument ceremony, church members eagerly held their own foundation stone celebration, and gleefully placed underneath it a vessel containing, among other items, the first issue of the *Colonial Advocate*.[123]

Scolding the Elite

From the start, the *Advocate* editor was most effective when on the attack, especially when he was attacking the oligarchy of officials and their friends who dominated the provincial political scene. This "York junta"

was the enemy of all he stood for. He scolded, he scoffed, he satirized –
even with poetry.

The second issue of the *Advocate* included a spoof on Solicitor General Henry J. Boulton who had just announced that he would stand for
election to the Assembly. Mackenzie's poem took the form of an address
to the electors whom Boulton wished to represent. Boulton sings:

> Dear Tom, and Dick, and Harry
> What makes you all so merry,
> At the expense of Solicitor Dandy O?
> Who wishes and who hopes
> You'll all prove such nincompoops
> As to swallow all his blarney and his brandy O!
>
> Prior to making my profession,
> I have waited a whole session,
> Ere I bolted out that I am so handy O!
> But see what a clever fellow
> Without "leather or prunella"
> Is your mixture of water and brandy O![124]

It continued on in this manner for sixteen more stanzas, such as:

> "Intelligence and zeal" for the public weal
> Marks every word and action of your Dandy O!
> Your little candidate, if you'll smile upon his fate;
> Will treat you with a drop of the Brandy O!
>
> If I do not you please,
> If you're very ill at ease
> With modest Harry B—lt—n, the dandy O;
> If I prove not firm and true
> To the Lawyer's oath and vow,
> I'll consent to shut my Gin Shop—save my Brandy O!

Many stanzas contained references to prominent men and issues of the
time, such as this one which referred to Fothergill, the *Gazette* editor, and
to George Boulton, Henry Boulton's brother (and fellow lawyer), who
were both running for the same Durham seat:

> If F— a new edition
> Of his Durhamshire petition
> 'Gainst I and brother Georgey should bandy O;
> I'll in family compact join,

Sir Peregrine Maitland

Brock's Monument

D'Arcy Boulton, Sr.

Henry John Boulton

John Strachan

John Beverley Robinson

> We will catch him at his wine
> And we'll keep in lawyer's tolls the Gazette randy O!

(This is the first known Canadian use of the phrase "family compact." As used here, it simply referred to the Boulton brothers being in league with each other and with their father D'Arcy Boulton, a justice of the Court of King's Bench. In later years, the term "Family Compact" would later gain wide currency, thanks especially to Mackenzie, as a derisive epithet for the provincial ruling élite, including, of course, the Boultons).

> Like Goessman, I'll not sell
> Nor buy your votes pell mell;
> It would not look well, nor be handy O!
> Of my blarney I am vogue
> For I've got none of the brogue,
> So when I've got your votes you'll have the Brandy O!

A few issues later, Mackenzie mocked, but with less hostility, another member of the establishment, William Allan, holder of a multitude of offices in York. The editor imagined a newcomer to town:

> A gentleman crossed to York from Oswego; on arriving at the little capital, he enquired for the customs house, as he had some goods aboard to enter at that office — he was shewn the place, hard by the quay. The COLLECTOR proved to be a very mild, good natured gentleman, as might be; a quiet man of business too, very conversant with figures … he was — Mr. William Allan. On opening his trunk, Mr. Z found some of his letters were to be left at the post-master of York; he enquired where it was located, and in the POST-MASTER recognized — Mr. William Allan. He has some bills which he wished to discount … [at] the Bank of Upper Canada — was shewn the president of that institution, and that PRESIDENT was the indefatigable — Mr. William Allan. A day or two after, he was accompanying a friend, who had come to town to pay some money for a store and tavern licence — on arriving at the office of the INSPECTOR OF LICENCES, he was amazed to find that functionary also in the person of — Mr. William Allan. A review of the militia took place while he stayed. He had the curiosity to go see it, and recognized in the COLONEL, his (now) old acquaintance — Mr. William Allan! A row took place in the hotel where he lodged; his evidence was wanted, and the acting MAGISTRATE was — Mr. William Allan! Taking up a newspaper to amuse himself, he read the name of the society for strangers in distress. The TREASURER was — Mr. William Allan!! Walking with a friend to see the hospital, he was told the name of the TRUSTEES. One

of them was — Mr. William Allan!! He happened to overhear a debate about a property which had been forfeited, by a man who ran away in the time of the war; the name of the COMMISSIONERS were mentioned … and one of them was — Mr. William Allan!! Another day he met a friend from Niagara in doleful mood, enquired the cause, and was informed that the COMMISSIONERS for war losses, had cut off half his claim. Who are the commissioners asked he of Oswego, the reply was A. B. C. D. and — Mr. William Allan!! He sold some of his goods to a merchant who gave him an order on the treasurer of the district — the TREASURER was — Mr. William Allan!! He could hold no longer; but amazed, astonished, and confounded, exclaimed, "How I pity this poor man, this Mr. William Allan; if he does the duty of so many different situations, his life must surely be a burden to himself; and if he does not, how I pity a country, the laws of which allow one man to hold such a number of important trusts at one time." "Poli!" says my uncle Sim, who lives near president Allan, on the same street, "you are a stranger and should be silent; you see but a small specimen of the blessings of our provincial government. The Colonel is … a Scotsman, you know … a favourite of the government … a real man of business, and worth a plum. In short, he is — he is — Mr. WILLIAM ALLAN!!!"

Mackenzie did not mean this teasing tale to be a personal attack. "It is not him of whom we complain; if any one ought to have fifty profitable trusts, he is the man but condemning favouritism as we do in principle."[125]

In his initial editorial, Mackenzie had promised that the columns of he paper would not all be deadly serious: "Satire properly directed is a most powerful weapon! How few can withstand it." He would quickly learn how truly he had written. Satirical barbs were taken personally and seriously. By the seventh issue of his paper, he felt compelled to declare, "when I am reduced to personalities, I will bring the Advocate to a close."[126]

(Two years later, the editor was indeed "reduced to personalities" in an especially satirical and thereby particularly offensive editorial commentary. It nearly brought the paper to a close, for it prompted a group of men to raid his office, damage his press and destroy much of his type.[127])

The 'Advocate' as a Newspaper

In the early months of its existence, the *Colonial Advocate* covered events in many other countries as well as the United States. By exchanging with other editors, Mackenzie had a ready source of foreign news. In the course of its first few months, he devoted space to happenings in Brazil, Mexico, Germany, Turkey, Greece, and, of course, Britain and its colonies.

Some news articles were several paragraphs in length. At other times Mackenzie compiled brief squibs as news one-liners. For example, headed "Miscellaneous Intelligence," in one issue he ran sixty-seven of them — accidents, weather reports, inventions, agricultural reports, deaths, political developments, shipping news and much more.[128] And nearly every paper's columns included brief anecdotes, poetic squibs, quotations, and other items of incidental interest, all culled from other papers.

The editor was never one to underestimate the value of his own advice. He even had the temerity to use the columns of the *Advocate* to address the editors of two New York newspapers from which, he acknowledged, he extracted much of his "foreign intelligence of importance." He had an idea, he dared "respectfully suggest," to improve their service. "Their Canadian readers" (were there many, other than Mackenzie himself?) would receive "great advantages" if Liverpool "agents" (the more modern newspaper term is "stringers") were appointed. These agents would then send "a private letter to the editor" via each outgoing ship "whither to New York, Boston, or Philadelphia." Thereby "much valuable advice" (that is, current news) "might be obtained ... which is not realized until much later, or not at all."[129] (What response, if any, he received from the two editors, he never reported.)

In the late summer, a court case in Newcastle roused his wrath. Ship captain William M'Intosh was prosecuted for an infraction of the customs laws. When the jury found for the defendant, Mr. Justice D'Arcy Boulton demanded, over strong objections from the defence lawyer, that the jury give written reasons for their verdict. He lectured them that the evidence was clear that the law had been broken. Prosecuting attorney Henry Boulton, provincial Solicitor General and the judge's son, also addressed the jury again, but no word was allowed for the defence. Again the jury found for the defendant. Again the judge demanded that they reconsider. Despite this intense judicial badgering, the jury held firm. Mackenzie voiced his indignation:

Were I at this moment immured in a dungeon, and denied the privileges
of the lowest hind that breathes the vital air, and crawls along, I would not
exchange places with our high born ruler, surrounded by such men as he
now delights to honor; no! I would spurn — I would loathe the very idea
of such prostration. I am the son of a humble, obscure mechanic, bred in
the lap of poverty; but not to inherit the noble blood which flows in his
veins — not to possess the ancestral grandeur that surrounds his name —
not to wear the star that adorns his breast, nor the honorable orders that
mark his valor — no! not for worlds would I exchange situations with
him, surrounded by men whose whole career is like 'vanity tossed to and
fro of them that seek death.'[130]

In the rhetorical style that later made him so effective at rousing the
populace he continued:

If a Judge can bully a Jury into submission, though expressly contrary to
their own solemn verdict; if a Solicitor for the Crown can trample under
foot the dearest rights of Britons; if a Government, emanating from England
can cherish such a corrupt, such a detestable star chamber crew — then we
may lament for ourselves, for our wives and our children that the British
Constitution is, in Canada, a phantom to delude to destruction, instead of
being the day star of our dearest liberties.[131]

When the assizes were held at Niagara, Mackenzie covered one trial
personally. It was a sad case indeed. The plaintiff, Fuller, sought damages
for "the loss of reputation and services of his daughter" from the defendant,
Secord, for fathering an illegitimate child. The evidence presented
showed that the parents were not only aware that their daughter and the
defendant "went regularly to bed," they did not discourage them.
According to the judge, there thus were no grounds for damages, and the
jury agreed. Mackenzie objected that "Mr. Justice Boulton's charge"
had made "the court smile often" about a case which ought not "provoke
any feelings than those of sorrow." The reporter's sympathies were for the

modest looking pale young woman, with more of simplicity in her looks
and manner than I can describe…. Though I acquiesce in the justice of
the verdict that was given against her, I would hope and trust that Mr.
Secord will not suffer her to be in want. One of the country people whom
I saw since, told me he met the poor thing going home by herself, her little
baby in her arms, through the swamp, barefooted and sobbing bitterly.

But the bulk of his report – a full newspaper column – was directed
against the failure of the church to send ministers into the "extensive
vineyard which this country offers" to preach and teach.

> If this girl, if her father, if her mother, had known the work of truth…had
> been under the influence of a gospel ministry; had lived where the example
> of an evangelical priest was made manifest, I am convinced, both from the
> countenance of the lass herself, her testimony, the appearance of her aged
> parent, and what I heard out of court, that the disclosures she made, which
> are a disgrace to the country (the more so from the plainness, the simplicity,
> with which she spoke) would never have shocked a Niagara audience.

His attack was against the established Church of England and Presbyterian Church of Scotland. He had nothing but praise for the Methodist Clergy. Were it not for them,

> where would this country be? They go to the woods and forests, to the
> most secluded and remote dwellings of man; and wherever they find two
> or three gathered together, there are they, ready to sing the praises of God,
> and to expound his word.[132]

On another occasion, protesting another matter, he wrote (as he would so often throughout his editorial career) in the language of an orating preacher himself:

> Canadians! The cause of the oppressor can never be yours. Scotsmen!
> Wallace resisted tyranny and oppression even until death. Englishmen!
> Hampden died on the field, and Sydney gave his life upon the scaffold,
> to perpetuate your liberties. Irishmen! remember the country you left
> behind, ponder upon its ruined commerce, its unhappy factions, its
> infesting divisions, and its prostrate hopes. Instruct your chosen ones to
> rise up in their might against those who would make Canada the sport
> and derision of the nations — who would trample on you until you
> could no longer feel their cruelty. Tell your senators to exercise their
> undoubted unalienable right to dismiss from his presence and counsel,
> John Beverley Robinson, and the whole of the Boulton race, root and
> branch forever.[133]

That summer of 1824, Robert Gourlay's name was back in the news. As we have seen, the treatment of Gourlay by members of the government establishment conditioned their attitudes toward Mackenzie. In 1817 Gourlay had come to Upper Canada to learn about its economic and political climate prior to promoting a scheme for emigration from Britain. What he discovered prompted him to urge a number of reforms. The official response was not to answer him but to eliminate him. He was arrested on questionable charges, jailed for several months until his health broke, and then banished.[134] Memories of his ideas and of his treatment lived on in the minds of anyone who continued to be dissatisfied with the Upper Canada political status quo.

The "Banished Briton"[135] was receiving renewed notice (or notoriety, depending on one's political leanings) in 1824 for an incident at the British House of Commons. The *Advocate's* pages reported details, quoted letters, published petitions, and reminded readers of past injustices.

Printing the 'Colonial Advocate'

The fearless *Advocate* publisher soon claimed he was printing "upwards of 1,000 copies." This was "more than one third of all the papers printed in the Province," he boasted, and produced the figures: *U.C. Gazette* 800; *Observer* 290; *Kingston Chronicle* 350; *Kingston Herald* 420; *Brockville Recorder* 300; *Niagara Gleaner* 190.[136] The *Gleaner* immediately complained that its numbers had been grossly underestimated.[137]

The first two issues of the *Advocate* were produced in pamphlet form, sixteen pages each, with covers of four more pages. By number three Mackenzie had switched to a five-column broadsheet, four page folio. Whether he realized it or not, the change to a broadsheet format signified that his journal was indeed a *news* paper, focused on whatever was new and news.

The first few issues were essentially long essays, outlining Mackenzie's opinions and imparting agricultural information. He initially expected to produce a respected, high-toned journal, but the vehemence of his editorial expression and the economics of publishing and circulating a paper quickly got in the way. The very factors which attracted public attention – independence and controversy – may have deterred some advertisers who merely wanted to sell their goods or services. Nevertheless, within a few weeks more than a quarter of the paper's space was taken up by advertising. The paper was clearly beginning to pay for itself.

After he had put out four papers, the press was silent for three weeks. He skipped issues five and six, apologizing in number seven that he suffered from "prolonged ill health." (Perhaps he had discovered, along with every other editor of a weekly paper, that it is one thing to publish a paper, it is another to put one out every week. There would be publishing delays and missed deadlines throughout his journalistic career – some caused by physical illness, some by fiscal weakness. His problems were not unique – most editors in Upper Canada experienced similar publishing difficulties.) He promised to publish the two missing numbers later.

The English common press which presently stands at the Mackenzie Heritage Printery Museum in Queenston, Ontario. This press is commonly known as the "'Louis Roy Press" in honour of the King's printer who first printed the Upper Canada Gazette.

The ruins of Mackenzie's Queenston home prior to restoration.

Mackenzie's home as it now stands — the present home of the Mackenzie Heritage Printery Museum.

When number six finally did come out, in pamphlet form, near the end of September, much of it was taken up by an essay on canals. That *Advocate* issue ended with a ringing affirmation:

That Canada may flourish — that her roads and canals, her trade and commerce, her agriculture and manufactures, may make her the envy and admiration of the world — and that I may live to see her people free, prosperous, and contented, is the heart-felt wish of the Editor of the Advocate.[138]

The only printing press in the Niagara region, indeed one of only six in the entire province, was owned by Andrew Heron, editor/publisher of the *Gleaner*, with which the *Advocate* was in direct competition. At first Mackenzie had his paper printed across the river by Oliver Grace,[139] who produced the *Lewiston* [New York] *Democrat*. (Working in Grace's shop was Bartemas Ferguson, the printer once jailed in Upper Canada for publishing Robert Gourlay's letters.[140]) Heron immediately pounced on the sin of Mackenzie's cross-border shopping:

We…hope the Editor of the Advocate…will be a great gainer, even after paying the duty, and at the same time benefit his friends in the United States, by circulating a little of Canada Cash amongst his Cronies.[141]

In August Mackenzie contracted with a Rochester, New York printer, Hiram Leavenworth, to sell him his Ramage press and come with it to Queenston.[142] This meant the *Advocate* office could also do job printing even before it was ready to print the newspaper. Printing forms, letterheads and advertising circulars meant additional income. The general store was also still in business. (It is not recorded how Mackenzie's family reacted to their home being turned into a printshop as well as a store and an editorial office.)

Alas, no financial records of the *Advocate* are extant (most of Mackenzie's papers were lost or destroyed at the time of the Rebellion). It is not known how much job printing was actually done. In September Captain John Matthews ordered two hundred copies of a political broadside.[143] A month or so later, Drs. Charles Duncombe and John Rolph paid for fliers promoting their new St. Thomas Medical School.[144]

By late September, the Queenston shop began printing the newspaper. Mackenzie delighted that number fifteen of the *Advocate* was "as rare a curiosity as any newspaper that ever was printed in the world! The first side was printed in the American Republick, and this in the Colonial Dominions of King George 4th."[145]

This new arrangement did not silence the *Advocate*'s critics, however. An Ancaster poet, pseudonym "Croaker," produced for the *Gleaner*, "The Two Sided Paper" which read in part:

You will *distract* your readers, great Sir Mac,
If thus you stories tell, and gibes you crack;
E'n now they are half Yankee, half Canadian,
And cry "vive la Republique," and "God save Sir Peregrine."
This comes of reading your two-sided paper,
And raising such a mighty cloud of vapour,
About the mighty men, and powers that be,
The men, who, under God, direct our destiny.—
One reads *this* side, and cries "God save the King,"
Then reads the *other* and cries "no such thing;"
Thus does he damn alternately and save
This Lord and that (a base two-sided knave;)
Now clapping hands for *this*, perhaps with reason,
Now swearing *that* is spiced with blood and treason;
And all brought on by *thee*, thou turn-coat mongrel,
Whose real name is said to be Mac S__nd__l.[146]

When "A Friend" wrote to complain about the paper's style and grammar, the editor confessed: "We very seldom read what we write until we receive, from the printer for correction, the proof sheet."[147]

Personal Life

Mackenzie rarely paraded personal matters before his readers; his private life was essentially that, private. Even his personal reminiscences were largely for the purpose of political argument. He referred, as we have seen, to his mother's courage during his childhood poverty, but he gave little evidence of his current economic condition, save to say "We are not in want, neither are we rich." In an early request for payments for ads and subscriptions, he did mention that in "only one instance in our past did we ever prosecute for debt."[148] When fellow editors Carey and Heron charged that he had received special treatment from the government by being given ten building lots when he lived in Dundas, he denied it vigorously. "I got one lot on condition of building a frame house" and paying a fee of $30. The other lots he owned there had been sold to him.[149]

Only occasional references offer glimpses into his domestic existence. In one issue the family advertised for a maid servant, "a Scotch woman would be preferred."[150] In October he advertised that the Mackenzie family would need sixty cords of wood for the winter.[151] The editor travelled widely, leaving his family for days at a time – on one trip he lost "a Red Morocco Pocketbook containing notes and papers."[152]

The Mackenzie family home was located with his business in a stone house near the foot of Queenston Heights,[153] site of the famous War of 1812 battle. The household consisted of his wife of two years; their baby daughter (born in Dundas shortly before the move to Queenston), his seventy-five year old mother, and his son, by then ten years old.[154] In September a second daughter was born – she lived only a few hours and was buried, unbaptized, in the Stamford church burying ground.[155] Mackenzie printed no notice in his newspaper.

The fourth issue of the *Advocate* included some wise words – written by the editor or quoted from an unknown source – which may be read as a tribute to his wife, Isabel Baxter Mackenzie:

> No man ever prospered in this world without the consent and co-operation
> of his wife. If she unites in mutual endeavours, or rewards his labour with
> an endearing smile, with what perseverance does he apply to his vocation![156]

The family often attended services at the Presbyterian church in nearby Stamford (now part of Niagara Falls). In one issue of the paper he described in detail a special communion celebration held there. His commentary included several detailed comparisons as to the similarities and the differences between the scene at this Stamford church and one held in Scotland. The editor was clearly familiar with hymnody and church choral music and he could favorably review the content of the preaching. He could not, however, write for two and half columns without making passing political reference to the son of the Lieutenant-Governor (the Maitland family resided much of the year on an estate in Stamford) passing by without stopping.[157]

In November, 1824, Mackenzie moved family and printing establishment to the provincial capital of York. The decision to move was apparently made rather suddenly. Not only had he advertised a need for wood, as we have seen, in late October he had advertised for a "steady compositor, accustomed to set from manuscript" and for two lads to serve as apprentices in the *Advocate* printing office.[158] What prompted the move is not clear, but apart from printing, competition in Queenston had increased – there were five stores whereas a year earlier that had been but one.[159]

Politically, the move was appropriate. To be considered a major actor on the political stage, he had to move from the periphery to the centre, where the government was. And the new session of Parliament, with many changes in its membership as a result of the summer elections, was about to begin.

One sad consequence of this move was the death a few weeks later of daughter Isabel. The grieving father recorded in the family Bible: "She was a lovely child, and caught the small pox, on the voyage from Queenston to York (as we think)."[160]

Afterword

In his last Queenston number, Mackenzie confessed:

> I am aware that the Advocate has fallen far short of the expectations that were formed from the promises made in my first number. It has degenerated into an ordinary provincial newspaper, of the smallest size — it is printed on coarser paper, and with a type much larger than the work it professed to copy.[161] I am sorry the province will not support one newspaper of the size of the United States country weekly journals, but so it is. There is not, as far as I can learn, one journal in Upper Canada, whether servile or independent in politics; the proprietors of which can boast that it is at all a profitable concern in the mercantile sense of the word.[162]

Despite the editor's misgivings, however, the *Colonial Advocate* changed the political landscape of Upper Canada. Because of Mackenzie's vigorous commentary, the province would never be the same again. From the 1824 publication of the *Advocate* to the 1837 rallying of rebels at Montgomery's Tavern runs a single strand. It ended in a Toronto winter – if it ended at all – but it began in a Queenston spring.

The day he launched the *Colonial Advocate*, in front of his Queenston house Mackenzie planted a row of locust trees. More than thirty years later, after publishing the *Advocate* for ten years followed by *The Constitution* for two, after his tumultuous career in the House of Assembly, after serving as first mayor of Toronto, after leading the ill-fated Rebellion, after escaping to the United States and living there in exile, after returning to Canada and restarting life as an editor and as a politician, he revisited Queenston. He noted that his trees had "grown luxuriously." He had originally planted them, he wrote, "to commemorate the day that had transformed a quiet, peaceful obscure trader into an ardent colonial politician and public censor."[163] One hundred and seventy-five years later, two of these trees still stand.

Appendix: Mackenzie Genealogy

The Genealogy of William Lyon Mackenzie

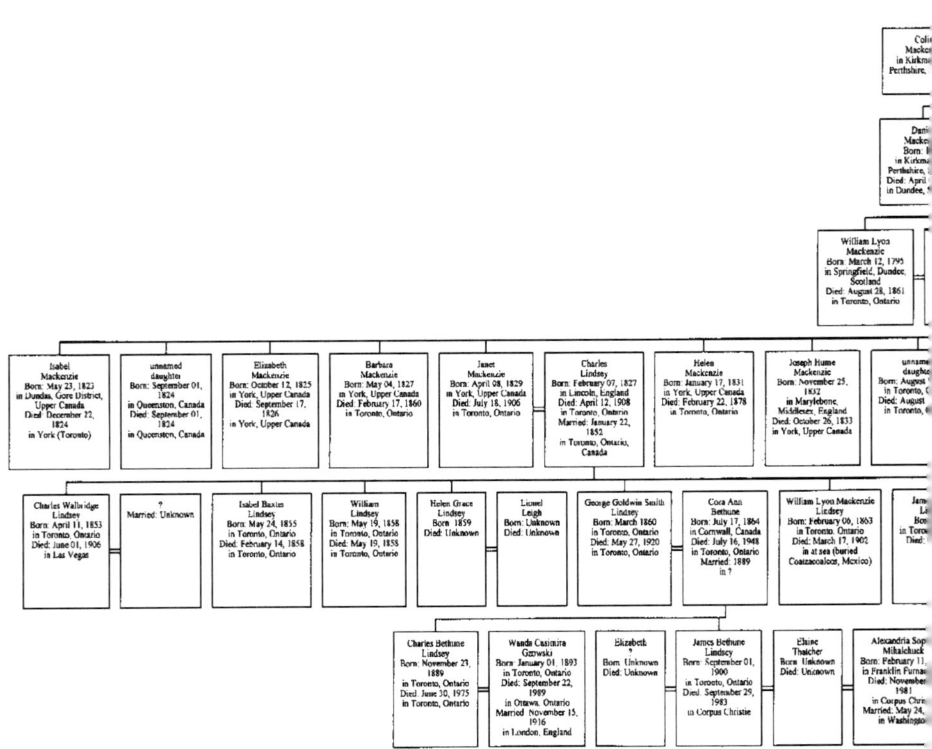

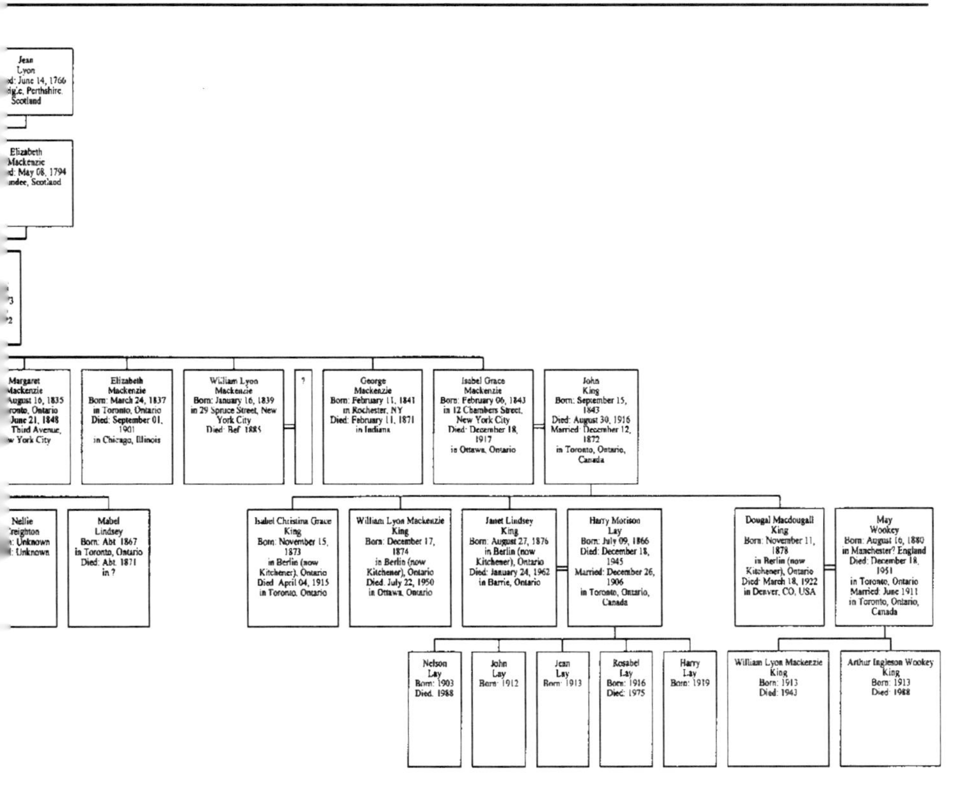

Jean
Lyon
d: June 14, 1766
...gie, Perthshire,
Scotland

Elizabeth
Mackenzie
d: May 08, 1794
...ndee, Scotland

3
2

Margaret
Mackenzie
August 16, 1835
...ronto, Ontario
June 21, 1848
Third Avenue,
...w York City

Elizabeth
Mackenzie
Born: March 24, 1837
in Toronto, Ontario
Died: September 01,
1901
in Chicago, Illinois

William Lyon
Mackenzie
Born: January 16, 1839
in 29 Spruce Street, New
York City
Died: Bef 1885

?

George
Mackenzie
Born: February 11, 1841
in Rochester, NY
Died: February 11, 1871
in Indiana

Isabel Grace
Mackenzie
Born: February 06, 1843
in 12 Chambers Street,
New York City
Died: December 18,
1917
in Ottawa, Ontario

John
King
Born: September 15,
1843
Died: August 30, 1916
Married: December 12,
1872
in Toronto, Ontario,
Canada

Nellie
Creighton
n: Unknown
d: Unknown

Mabel
Lindsey
Born: Abt 1867
in Toronto, Ontario
Died: Abt 1871
in ?

Isabel Christina Grace
King
Born: November 15,
1873
in Berlin (now
Kitchener), Ontario
Died: April 04, 1915
in Toronto, Ontario

William Lyon Mackenzie
King
Born: December 17,
1874
in Berlin (now
Kitchener), Ontario
Died: July 22, 1950
in Ottawa, Ontario

Janet Lindsey
King
Born: August 27, 1876
in Berlin (now
Kitchener), Ontario
Died: January 24, 1962
in Barrie, Ontario

Harry Morison
Lay
Born: July 09, 1866
Died: December 18,
1945
Married: December 26,
1906
in Toronto, Ontario,
Canada

Dougal Macdougall
King
Born: November 11,
1878
in Berlin (now
Kitchener), Ontario
Died: March 18, 1922
in Denver, CO, USA

May
Wookey
Born: August 16, 1880
in Manchester? England
Died: December 18,
1951
in Toronto, Ontario
Married: June 1911
in Toronto, Ontario,
Canada

Nelson
Lay
Born: 1903
Died: 1988

John
Lay
Born: 1912

Jean
Lay
Born: 1913

Rosabel
Lay
Born: 1916
Died: 1975

Harry
Lay
Born: 1919

William Lyon Mackenzie
King
Born: 1913
Died: 1943

Arthur Ingleson Wookey
King
Born: 1913
Died: 1988

Endnotes

1. Unless otherwise noted, quotations are from the *Colonial Advocate*, 1824 May 18.

2. Charles Lindsey, *The Life and Times of William Lyon Mackenzie,* Toronto: P.R. Randall, 1862, p. 48.

3. He announced his intention in *Mackenzie's Weekly Gazette,* 1839 September 08.

4. Unless otherwise noted, biographical details are from Charles Lindsey, *The Life and Times of William Lyon Mackenzie,* Toronto: P.R. Randall, 1862. Other biographies include: Frederick Armstrong and Ronald Stagg, "Mackenzie, William Lyon" in the *Dictionary of Canadian Biography, Vol. IX,* Toronto: University of Toronto Press, 1976; David Flint, *William Lyon Mackenzie: Rebel Against Authority,* Toronto: University of Toronto Press, 1971; Lillian F. Gates, *After the Rebellion: The Later Years of William Lyon Mackenzie,* Toronto: Dundurn Press, 1988; William Kilbourn, *The Firebrand,* Toronto: Clark Irwin, 1956; William Dawson LeSueur, *William Lyon Mackenzie: A Reinterpretation,* Toronto: Macmillan, 1971 (originally written ca. 1908); and Chris Raible, *Muddy York Mud: Scandal and Scurrility in Upper Canada,* Creemore: Curiosity House, 1992. See also the *Makers of Canada* edition of Charles Lindsey's work, retitled *William Lyon Mackenzie,* "Edited with Numerous Additions" by [son] G.G.S. Lindsey, Toronto: Morang, 1908.

5. F.K. Donnelly, "The British Background of William Lyon Mackenzie," *British Journal of Canadian Studies,* Vol. 2, #1, 1987.

6. Printed poster, quoted in Charles Lindsey, *The Life and Times of William Lyon Mackenzie,* Toronto: P.R. Randall, 1862, pp. 36-7.

7. Letter: James Mackenzie to Janet Mackenzie, 1885 November 22, William Lyon Mackenzie Collection, National Archives of Canada, vol. 9.

8. The formal dissolution documents are dated March 20, 1823.

9. For an account of the life of James Mackenzie, see Chris Raible, "Son of the Firebrand: James Mackenzie," *The Beaver,* 71.5, Sept.-Oct. 1991. A shorter version of the same story is in R. B. Fleming, ed., *Boswell's Children: The Art of the Biographer,* Chapter 8.

10. *Gleaner,* 1823 December 04.

11. Letters: Thomas Fyfe to William Lyon Mackenzie, 1824 January 28, February 06, March 13, May 13, June 05 in Mackenzie Correspondence, Mackenzie-Lindsey Papers, Archives of Ontario.

12. See, for example, Mackenzie's *Welland Canal* newspaper, three issues of which were published in December, 1835 to expose financial mismanagement of the canal.

13. Most of Mackenzie's personal papers were lost in the Rebellion. Some of his account books for his Toronto newspaper in the 1850s are in the Mackenzie-Lindsey Papers in the Archives of Ontario.

14. Andrew Murray Scott, *Discovering Dundee: The Story of a City*, Dundee: Mercat Press, 1989.

15. F. K. Donnelly, "The British Background of William Lyon Mackenzie," *British Journal of Canadian Studies*, Vol. 2, #1, 1987.

16. Letter to Randal Wixon, *Colonial Advocate*, 1833 June 20.

17. *Mackenzie's Weekly Message*, 1859 July 23.

18. Henry Hunt, William Cobbett (1763-1835), and James Watson.

19. *Colonial Advocate*, 1825 January 13.

20. *Mackenzie's Weekly Message*, 1860 March 17.

21. *Colonial Advocate*, 1824 June 03.

22. *Mackenzie's Weekly Message*, 1854 February 10.

23. Charles Lindsey, *The Life and Times of William Lyon Mackenzie*, Toronto: P.R. Randall, 1862, Appendix A, lists them all.

24. F. K. Donnelly, "The British Background of William Lyon Mackenzie," *British Journal of Canadian Studies*, Vol. 2, #1, 1987.

25. Frederick Armstrong & Ronald J. Stagg, "Mackenzie, William Lyon" in the *Dictionary of Canadian Biography, Vol. IX,* Toronto: University of Toronto Press, 1976.

26. Referred to in *Colonial Advocate*, 1824 December 16. No copy of the article has ever been located.

27. Frederick Armstrong & Ronald J. Stagg, "Mackenzie, William Lyon" *Dictionary of Canadian Biography, Vol. IX,* Toronto: University of Toronto Press, 1976. I found no "Mercator" in the few surviving issues of the *Observer.*

28. There are two anthologies of Mackenzie's writings: Margaret Fairley (ed.), *The Selected Writings of William Lyon Mackenzie: 1824-1837,* Toronto: Oxford University Press, 1960; and Anthony W. Rasporich (ed.), *William Lyon Mackenzie,* Canadian History through the Press Series, Toronto: Holt, Rinehart and Winston, 1972.

29. Henry Bathurst (1762–1834), British Colonial Secretary.

30. James Macintosh (1765–1832), Scottish philosopher & historian.

31. François René Chateaubriand (1768–1848), French writer & statesman.

32. Joseph Hume (1777-1855), English physician & radical politician, known as "Adversity Hume."

33. Henry Richard Vassail Fox (1773-1840), Baron Holland, British statesman.

34. John Gladstone, prominent British merchant and politician, father of William Gladstone, later Prime Minister.

35. George Canning (1770-1827), Foreign Secretary, later Prime Minister.

36. Thomas Chalmers (1780-1847), prominent Scottish theologian & preacher.

37. Frederick John Robinson, Viscount Goodrich & Earl of Ripon (1782-1859), Chancellor of the Exchequer, later prime minister, later colonial secretary.

38. I am unable to identify – presumably a prominent Presbyterian minister.

39. Henry Peter Brougham, Lord Brougham and Vaux (1778-1868), Scottish jurist & political leader.

40. John Leslie (1766-1832), Scottish mathematician.

41. Alexander Baring (1774-1848), British financier, Lord Ashburton.

42. Francis Jeffrey (1773-1850), Scottish critic & jurist, editor *Edinburgh Review.*

43. Marie Joseph Paul Yves Roch Gilbert du Motier de Lafayette (1757-1834), French nobleman, hero of American Revolution.

44. François Alexandre Frédéric La Rochefoucauld-Laincourt, Duc de (1747-1827), French social reformer.

45. Charles William Stewart (1778-1854), British soldier & diplomat.

46. George Ramsay, 9th Earl of Dalhousie (1770-1838), one of Wellington's generals, Governor of Canada.

47. Peregrine Maitland (1777-1854), one of Wellington's generals, Lieutenant-Governor of Upper Canada.

48. I am unable to identify – presumably an active member of the House of Lords.

49. Thomas Makdougall Brisbane (1773-1860), British soldier & astronomer, Governor of New South Wales.

50. James Stuart (1780-1853), Attorney General of Lower Canada.

51. For details of the life of Robert Gourlay, see Lois Darroch Milani, *Robert Gourlay, Gadfly,* Toronto: Ampersand Press, 1971; S.F. Wise, "Gourlay, Robert," in the *Dictionary of Canadian Biography, Vol. IX; Toronto: University of Toronto Press, 1976* and William Renwick Riddell, "Robert (Fleming) Gourlay," *Ontario Historical Society Papers and Records, XIV* (1916).

52.James Monroe (1758-1851).

53.William Harris Crawford (1772-1834), American lawyer, candidate for president of the United States.

54.DeWitt Clinton (1769-1828), Governor of New York

55.Daniel Webster (1782-1852), U.S. Congressman, Massachusetts

56.Daniel D.Thompkins (1774-1825).

57.John Randolph (1773-1833), U.S. Congressman,Virginia

58.John Quincy Adams (1767-1848), U.S. Secretary of State – in 1825, U.S. President.

59.I am unable to identify – presumably a U.S. Congressman.

60.Henry Clay (1777-1852), U.S. Congressman, Kentucky; Speaker, U.S. House of Representatives.

61.*Weekly Register*, 1824 May 27.

62.*Colonial Advocate*, 1824 June 03.

63.See Milton W. Hamilton, *The Country Printer: New York State, 1785-1830, Second edition*. Port Washington, New York: Ira J. Friedman, 1964. (originally printed, Columbia University Press, 1936).

64.*Colonial Advocate*, 1824 July 29.

65.An iron smelting and casting operation, see Dianne Newell, *Technology on the Frontier: Mining in Old Ontario*. Vancouver, 1986.

66.For a description of his filing system, see Chris Raible, "'Consulting Authorities Continually, So Many Are My Imperfections'William Lyon Mackenzie As Editor and Publisher." *Ex Libris News*, No. 15 (Spring 1994).

67.Brian Tobin, *The* Upper Canada Gazette *and its printers, 1793-1849*. Toronto: Ontario Legislative Library,   .

68.Robert Charles Horne, editor *Upper Canada Gazette*, 1817–1821.

69.For an account of the trials and tribulations of early Canadian printers, see Chris Raible, "A Printer is Indispensably Necessary," *The Beaver* 77.4, Aug.–Sept. 1997.

70.See Elwood H. Jones "Willcocks, Joseph" in the *Dictionary of Canadian Biography, Vol. V*. Toronto University of Toronto Press, 1983.

71.See Robert Lachiel Fraser "Ferguson, Bartemas" in the *Dictionary of Canadian Biography, Vol. VI*; Toronto: University of Toronto Press, 1987; also Chris Raible, *Muddy York Mud: Scandal and Scurrility in Upper Canada*. Creemore, Ontario: Curiosity House, 1992, chapter 6.

72.See Elizabeth Hulse, "Newspapers" in Patricia Fleming, *Upper Canada Imprints 1800-1841*. Toronto: University of Toronto Press 1988.

73. See Elizabeth Hulse, "Newspapers" in Patricia Fleming, *Upper Canada Imprints 1800-1841.* Toronto: University of Toronto Press 1988.

74. William Lyon Mackenzie, *Sketches of Upper Canada,* London: 1833.

75. *Colonial Advocate,* 1824 July 08.

76. *Colonial Advocate,* 1824 July 08

77. Population statistics for Upper Canada are tabulated in Frederick H. Armstrong, ed., *Handbook of Upper Canadian Chronology, revised edition.* Toronto: Dundurn Press, 1985, p. 275.

78. Quoted in Gerald M Craig, *Upper Canada: The Formative Years 1784-1841.* Toronto: McClelland & Stewart, 1963. page 145.

79. *Upper Canada Gazette* and *Weekly Register,* 1824 June 03.

80. See Alan Wilson, *The Clergy Reserves of Upper Canada, A Canadian Mortmain,* Toronto: University of Toronto Press 1968.

81. See G. M. Craig, "Strachan, John" in the *Dictionary of Canadian Biography, Vol. IX,* Toronto: University of Toronto Press, 1976.

82. William Pitt, Earl of Chatham (1708-1778), English statesman.

83. *Colonial Advocate,* 1824 June 10.

84. Joseph Addison (1672-1719), English essayist.

85. *A Visit to the Province of Upper Canada in 1819,* published in England in 1820, by James Strachan – likely ghost written by his brother, the Rev. Dr. John Strachan.

86. Hugh Blair (1718-1800), Scottish Presbyterian clergyman and/or Robert Blair (1699-1746) Scottish clergyman.

87. François de Salignac de La Mothe-Fénelon (1651-1715), French prelate and writer.

88. Probably Thomas Erskine, Baron Erskine of Restormel (1750-1823), eminent British advocate.

89. Samuel Romilly (1757-1818), English lawyer and law reformer.

90. William Pitt, Earl of Chatham (1708-1778) and son William Pitt (1759-1806), English statesmen.

91. Henry Fox, Baron Holland (1705-1774), British statesman, among other Foxes.

92. George Canning (1770-1827), British statesman.

93. DeWitt Clinton (1769-1828), Governor of New York.

94. Probably John Moore (1761-1809), British General.

95. George Washington (1732-1799), first president of the United States.

96. Horatio Nelson, Viscount Nelson (1758-1805), British naval hero.

97. Adam Duncan, Viscount Duncan of Camperdown (1731-1804), British naval commander.

98. Edmund Burke (1729-1797), British statesman.

99. Probably Richard Brinsley Sheridan (1751-1816), Irish dramatist and orator.

100. Henry Peter Brougham, Baron of Brougham and Vaux (1778-1868), Scottish jurist and political leader.

101. Sir Francis Baring (1740-1810) and son Alexander Baring, Baron Ashburton (1774-1848), British financiers.

102. Address at the closing of the first session of the first Parliament of Upper Canada, 1792 October 15.

103. "…he that hateth covetousness shall prolong his days" – Proverbs 28:16

104. My own examination of copies of the first two issue of the *Advocate* (held by the Archives of Ontario) confirm that the fibres of the cover stock are pale blue, giving the cover a faint blue hue, in contrast to the uncoloured stock of the body of the newspaper itself.

105. See Robert Lochiel Fraser, "Nichol, Robert" in the *Dictionary of Canadian Biography, Vol. VI.* Toronto: University of Toronto Press, 1987.

106. *Weekly Register* (editorial supplement to the *Upper Canada Gazette*) 1824 May 27.

107. *Weekly Register,* 1824 June 03.

108. Robinson to Hillier, 1824 May 19, Upper Canada Sundries.

109. *Colonial Advocate,* 1824 June 03.

110. *Weekly Register,* 1824 June 03.

111. *Colonial Advocate,* 1824 June 10.

112. *Colonial Advocate,* 1824 June 10.

113. *Gleaner,* 1824 October 09. Mackenzie was of slight build.

114. *Colonial Advocate,* 1824 August 19.

115. *Colonial Advocate,* 1824 August 19.

116. *Gleaner,* 1824 October 09.

117. *Colonial Advocate,* 1824 October 02.

118. *Canadian Review,* Vol. 1, 1824 July, p. 216.

119. *Colonial Advocate,* 1824 June 03 and 10.

120. *Colonial Advocate,* 1824 July 08.

121. John Charles Dent, *The Story of the Upper Canadian Rebellion,* Toronto: C. Blackett Robinson, 1885, Vol. 1, pp. 122-123.

122. *Colonial Advocate* 1824 September 30. See also Patricia Fleming, *Upper Canadian Imprints 1801-1841*, Toronto: University of Toronto Press, 1988, p. 66.

123. *Colonial Advocate,* 1824 July 23.

124. *Colonial Advocate,* 1824 May 27.

125. *Colonial Advocate* 1824 August 19.

126. *Colonial Advocate* 1824 July 01.

127. For the full story of the "types riot" and its aftermath, see Chris Raible, *Muddy York Mud: Scandal and Scurrility in Upper Canada*, Creemore: Curiosity House, 1992.

128. *Colonial Advocate,* 1824 August 19.

129. *Colonial Advocate,* 1824 October 14.

130. "The getting of treasures by a lying tongue is a vanity tossed to and fro of them that seek death." – Proverbs 21:6.

131. *Observer,* reprinted in *Colonial Advocate,* 1824 November 04.

132. *Colonial Advocate,* 1824 August 19.

133. *Colonial Advocate,* 1824 October 28.

134. For details of the life of Robert Gourlay, see Lois Darroch Milani, *Robert Gourlay, Gadfly,* Toronto: Ampersand Press, 1971; S.F. Wise, "Gourlay, Robert" *Dictionary of Canadian Biography, Vol. IX;* Toronto: University of Toronto Press, 1976 and William Renwick Riddell, "Robert (Fleming) Gourlay," *Ontario Historical Society Papers and Records, XIV* (1916).

135. The title of a book by Gourlay published in 1837.

136. *Colonial Advocate,* 1824 August 05.

137. *Gleaner,* 1824 August 21.

138. *Colonial Advocate,* 1824 September 27.

139. *Mackenzie's Weekly Message,* 1855 December 07.

140. See Chris Raible, *Muddy York Mud: Scandal and Scurrility in Upper Canada.* Creemore, Ontario: Curiosity House, 1992, chapter 6; and Robert Lochiel Fraser, "Ferguson, Bartemas" in the *Dictionary of Canadian Biography, Vol. VI,* Toronto: University of Toronto Press: 1987.

141. *Gleaner,* 1824 May 19 and June 12.

142. "Agreement for Six Months With Bond Between Hiram Leavenworth of Rochester and Wm. L. Mackenzie of Queenston" 1824 August 24. Published: *Niagara Historical Society Transactions,* No. 30, 1917.

143. John Matthews to W.L. Mackenzie, 1824 September 30 and October 24 – Mackenzie-Lindsey Papers, Archives of Ontario.

144.Charles Duncombe to W. L. Mackenzie. November 20 – Mackenzie-Lindsey Papers, Archives of Ontario.

145.*Colonial Advocate,* 1824 October 07.

146.*Gleaner,* 1824 October 1824.

147.*Colonial Advocate,* 1824 June 03.

148.*Colonial Advocate,* 1824 June 10.

149.*Colonial Advocate,* 1824 July 29.

150.*Colonial Advocate,* 1824 June 03.

151.*Colonial Advocate,* 1824 October 21.

152.*Colonial Advocate,* 1824 July 29.

153.The house was restored in the 1930s and is now owned by the Niagara Parks Commission.

154.For more details of the Mackenzie family life, see Nancy Luno, *A Genteel Exterior: The Domestic Life of William Lyon Mackenzie and his Family,* Toronto: Toronto Historical Board, 1990.

155.Inscription in the Mackenzie Family Bible, in the possession of the Toronto Historical Board.

156.*Colonial Advocate,* 1824 June 10.

157.*Colonial Advocate,* 1824 August 26.

158.*Colonial Advocate,* 1824 October 28.

159.*Colonial Advocate,* 1824 September 02.

160.Inscription in the Mackenzie Family Bible, in the possession of the Toronto Historical Board.

161.It is not clear what paper he had in mind – possibly William Cobbett's *Political Register.*

162. *Colonial Advocate,* 1824 November 18.

163. *Mackenzie's Weekly Message,* 1854 May 19.

Colophon

THIS TEXT OF THIS BOOK was set in Bembo. The type was originally designed by early-Venetian printer and publisher Aldus Manutius for use in his 1495 edition of *De Aetna* by Cardinal Bembo from which it takes its name. The type was updated and reissued for machine composition in the 1920s by the Monotype Corporation. The titles are set in Caslon Open Face, one of the large selection of types from the famous Caslon Type Foundry created in 1722-3 by William Caslon in London, England. William Lyon Mackenzie himself imported Caslon-designed types from a foundry in New York to set the *Colonial Advocate*.